Complete Field Guide to Successful Sales Leadership

Your Path to Understanding How to Win at Results-Based Leadership

CHUCK THOKEY

COMPLETE FIELD GUIDE TO SUCCESSFUL SALES LEADERSHIP
Your Path to Understanding How to Win at Results-Based Leadership

Published by:
ThoughtLeaderPress.com

First Edition

Ebook ISBN: 978-1-61343-191-7

Paperback ISBN: 978-1-61343-190-0

Hardcover ISBN: 978-1-61343-189-4

To my wife, Christina, you have been my most profound inspiration and greatest supporter. You push me every day to be a better version of myself.

To my parents, Larry & Cheryl, who gave me the gift of dreams and the ability to realize them.

To my children, Grace, Danny, Charlotte, and Cara, you continue to inspire and challenge me to make a difference in others.

TABLE OF CONTENTS

Foreword .... **vi**

Introduction .... **xiv**

CHAPTER 1: Sales Leadership 101 .... **24**

- Build the Machine 33
- Know the Numbers 35
- Fire Them All 39
- Make Up for Your Weaknesses 42
- That Small Piece 44
- Making Hard Decisions 46

CHAPTER 2: Do You Have What It Takes? **54**

- Are You Coachable? 60
- Are You Disciplined and Accountable? 64
- Are You Willing to Take a Call at Dinner? 68
- Sales Meetings: Are You Able to Engage Your Team? 71
- Are You Willing to Make Less Money? 76

CHAPTER 3: Recruiting: Drafting Your Players 80
What is Your Sales Culture? 90
How Do You Find Your Sales Reps? 92
How Do You Interview? 93
Setting Expectations For Sales Professionals 95
How Do You Assess Them? 96
How to Build a Strong Bench of Players 98
CHAPTER 4: Taking Over The Castle 106
Determining the Mission 115
Who Are You Bringing Onto Your Team? 118
Forecasting: Determining the Road Map 122
Celebrate, But Don't Exhale 126
CHAPTER 5: Greasing the Wheels 136
How to Fire Them Up 150
Tools for Success 152
Empathy versus Sympathy 154
If You Can Be Misunderstood, You Will Be 156
Lifelines 158
CHAPTER 6: Forecasting: The Crystal Ball 162
Knowing What You Want 173
Knowing Your Current KPIs 176
Breaking Down the Number 180
What Do You Do With the Numbers? 183
CHAPTER 7: Building Blocks: Sales Team Key Competencies 190
The Selling System 196
The Training Process 201
Key Competencies 204
Managing By Activities 205
Power Hour 207
Sales Meetings 210
Conclusion 214
About the Author 223

FOREWORD

by Brian Gottlieb

With its lakes and rivers, Wisconsin in the summertime offers a beautiful backdrop where people often enjoy weekends with a fishing pole in one hand and a good cigar in the other. It's a great state to raise a family and in 2009, it became the place where I started my business, Tundraland Home Improvements. I launched the business as a sunroom company from the back of a friend's warehouse, on a plastic folding table and $3,000 in cash.

I clearly remember those early days, dealing with long, brutally cold winter months when we didn't sell a single project. Those harsh months strained our cash flow and robbed me of many nights of sleep. It was clear to me that for the business to survive, I needed to pivot. And pivot we did.

In 2012, we diversified by starting a division of bath and shower remodeling. It wasn't nearly as popular as it is today. In fact, the concept of installing a shower in a day was practically unheard of. Fortunately, as we launched a shower business in Wisconsin, my friends who owned companies like Westshore Home, Reborn Cabinets, Newpro, Max Home, Fairbanks, and Alenco were doing the same in their states. And we were determined to figure this business out together.

We developed a friendly competition as we grew. Every month, we'd battle to top the leaderboard sent out by our bath manufacturer that reported on shower units sold. Some might have thought the competition was unfair as one friend joked, "Wisconsin has more cows than people!" In fact, our primary market had a population just shy of 200,000 people. Despite that, we competed just fine, selling and installing over 500 shower projects in a single month.

While others thought it impossible, our mantra was simple: "Who says we can't?"

It was an incredible time. We were close friends, learned from one another, and all grew our businesses together. We faced our struggles together and grew stronger because of it. In other words, we had a learning mindset.

Today, these organizations collectively generate over $2 billion in annual revenue.

I've also gained invaluable insights from visiting other companies and peeking behind the curtain of their operations. That's why our doors at Tundraland were always open as well. If someone from another company wanted a tour of our operation, I was more than happy to help.

And that's how I met Chuck Thokey.

At the time, Chuck was working with another bath company several states away and wanted to see how Tundraland functioned. Now, I've given plenty of tours in the past, but this one was different. The first thing that stood out to me was the unwavering commitment Chuck had to help that company grow – he was relentlessly determined to help them win. He wanted to see every aspect of the business and asked layered questions to fully understand not just my business, but how he could seamlessly integrate certain things we did into the organization he was helping. It didn't take me long to realize one thing: Chuck had a learning mindset.

The second thing that stood out to me was Chuck's love for the industry, and the eagerness he had to go back to the company he was helping and take action to improve it. His curiosity and passion for developing those around him revealed that he was far more than a 'consultant' or 'trainer'. He was a true high-performance coach.

Over the years I've watched with awe as he's grown his Top Rep training business, sharing strategy and best practices with countless people in this industry. I've referred many companies to his training programs and have always had amazing feedback from those individuals. I've also had the pleasure of seeing him speak on stage at the biggest industry events. Chuck lights up a room with his clarity of content, his discipline, his ability to connect with the audience, and his energy of enthusiasm. Today, Chuck's ripple effect in this industry goes far beyond those he teaches, trains, and coaches. He helps companies win. He helps managers win. He helps teams win. He helps the industry win.

When he showed me the first draft of the manuscript of this book, I loved it. He cleverly makes the case that if you want to build a high-performance sales team, you must start by building high-performance sales managers. He drills down on the mindset, the disciplines, and the behaviors needed to be a top manager in this business. He will challenge you to rethink what you stand for, and as a manager, what you simply can't tolerate. This book is more than just a sales guide.

It's a proven model to follow that when implemented, will take you and your team to a whole new level of success.

So, here's my suggestion for you. Grab a coffee or grab a cigar. But most importantly, grab a highlighter because this field training manual can fundamentally change the trajectory of your career, and those on your team.

Like my friends and I experienced as we grew our businesses together, and as Chuck demonstrates through his continued success, we are often surrounded by opportunities that can significantly transform our lives. However, these opportunities can easily slip by if we lack one very crucial element: a learning mindset. For the moment we think we know it all, it's probably time to retire.

Much love,

BG

Use the QR code to access all the documents referenced in this book. These are the same materials we share in our coaching sessions around the world, giving you practical tools to apply what you read and take real action.

INTRODUCTION

Let's be honest. Most sales leaders are lost.

I wasn't any different. When I first became a sales leader, I was looking for someone to help me, and tell me exactly what I was supposed to be doing. There were owners or others who would give advice, but they really didn't know what they were doing either.

I had to figure it out on my own, and it took a lot of sleepless nights, and a lot of, 'I am going to sleep for an hour and then try to get up and start working on my next sales meeting.'

I would think, 'These people keep telling me that I am supposed to manage by the numbers, so now

I have to try to figure out what numbers I am even supposed to manage by.'

I had to reach out for help, and I ended up finding mentors who changed everything for me. I would read a book and want to figure out who this person is, so I would research them to the point that I would track them down. I wanted to find out how they are so good in their field and learn from them. Doing this I gained access to the top coaches in the country. My first and most impactful coach was Keith Rosen, whom some would call the godfather of sales coaching. Keith wrote a book called "Coaching Salespeople Into Sales Champions." This was my coaching bible for many years.

One of my first mentors was from a company called 'Bath Fitter', and he was the VP of sales on the East Coast. His name was Frank. I would just sit back in awe, watching how direct and disciplined he was, and how the people who worked for him were so successful because of their accountability.

I then had the opportunity to learn from many other coaches and mentors for a few years and was able to take this information and help build an organization within 'Bath Fitter' where we grew at record speeds. I have used the training, coaching and mentorship to build many of the largest and most successful sales teams within the Home Services Industry around the world.

What I learned from these professionals, and now pass along to my own clients, is an understanding of sales leadership that is about results.

Results-based leadership is when you need results now, and not about rallying a team behind you and at some point being successful.

Success has to be brought daily, weekly, and monthly inside results-based leadership, and it is very fast-paced. There are no excuses!

It is a step-by-step understanding of the process of how to become a successful sales leader and a successful sales champion of a team.

Sales leaders are supposed to lead by example, but the problem is that most do not understand what that means.

They think that they are just going to sell and show their people that they know how to sell, which is not leading by example. Leading by example is showing them all the things that you want them to have, like having a good work ethic, and having discipline and having accountability. It also means that you already know, at an expert level, everything you plan to train the team. This enables them to understand what is expected of them.

Sales leaders are often on their own. Just yesterday, one of my sales reps decided that he was going to start his own organization. He told me, "It is really lonely out here. I have gotten rid of many of my friends because they were all negative. It is a lonely journey."

I told him, "It is lonely at the top. As you become that sales leader, people will stop hanging out with you as much because you just have so much going on. There is always something to be done. You don't have time to go out. You don't have time to meet people out very often. You are always planning for what is next."

As a sales leader, you need to understand what is expected of you in this rewarding position. You also need to understand the lives that you will have a chance to change.

My hope is that this book will be a bit of a flashlight on this journey, and help you to think about finding success inside an industry that has very little coaching and guidance.

Even for an experienced sales leader, there is always something to be learned. I have been doing this for over 20 years, and am still learning. If you are looking to grow in this industry of results-based sales or fast-paced sales, this will hopefully start to teach you the roadmap for making the organization a success.

When I got into this industry, I did not know anything, and I don't want anybody to have to go down the road that I went down. I was taking cold showers just to wake myself up because I couldn't sleep at night from the anxiety I had of knowing that I had to meet with ownership, knowing that I did not know what to tell them when we had a bad month. I knew that I could not make up excuses and that I needed to own up to everything that happened.

Sales leadership is like Mount Everest, some people make it, but most people don't. You learn as you go, and you decide if it is worth the pain.

In most cases, we get paid less than a lot of the sales reps, even though in many cases, we are better at sales than many of the sales reps.

So why do we become sales leaders? I believe that we make this conscious decision, so that we have the opportunity to change people's lives.

Why should you read anything I've written? Well, let me start at the beginning.

I grew up with severe learning disabilities, and I was not always in the same classes as a lot of my peers. It wasn't easy for me to learn in a school setting.

Later on, I had the opportunity to go into engineering. I went from having severe learning disabilities, to passing a test, to being among gifted students.

Long story short, it is not about what you can learn, it is what you are interested in. If you like what you are doing, you will do it twice as well. When I found what I liked doing, I did it better than anyone else.

I hate when people say, "Find your passion, and you'll never work a day in your life."

No, when you find your passion, you will work twice as hard every day of your life. Once I found out what it was that I liked to do, I excelled at it. I still graduated in the half of the class that made the top half possible, but graduated nonetheless. By the age of 19 or 20 years old, I was invited into the engineering department of Bombardier Learjet in Wichita, KS, making me one of the youngest aerospace engineers in the country.

I went from being labeled an idiot, to being labeled an aerospace engineer. Success is based on what it is that you love to do, and how badly you want it.

I look at this industry the same way. If you feel as though your purpose is in helping people realize that their life is about to change, that's a beautiful thing. And you can say that, because you know that you're about to help them change their lives, teaching them to be something that they never thought they could be. All of a sudden, you create the ability for them to find success.

Someone gave me that opportunity, and this is my opportunity to give back. So many people have poured information into me over the years, and now I am sharing their information and much of my knowledge gained through 20 years of experience with you.

You have the opportunity to be a champion, but no one can be a champion without someone teaching them and holding them accountable. The legacy is inside the long list of people whose lives have been changed.

These are people who never thought they could make more than $30-40k per year. These are people who never knew that they would work outside a car wash or a factory somewhere.

Because that sales leader took a chance on them, gave them knowledge, and showed them what they were supposed to do, they took them from a life of poverty that they were going to live, to now making $100-500k a year.

I hope that you can find a clearer path and have a different mindset as a sales leader. I want you to open your eyes and know where your next step is, and just how easy it can be.

It is funny because when I am off-stage, I don't talk much, but when I am on stage, I am very bold and direct. I have heard it many times when I get off the stage, the people who hear my speech say, "You are so intense, that was like 40 minutes of just being slapped in the face with what I should be doing."

I don't necessarily want to slap you in the face, but I want you to understand that if you truly want the success of your organization, you should want to grow the inside of your sales leadership team. Not just for the company, but for yourself to be a better leader. And for the amazing people who will become greater as a result of your efforts.

Think about your legacy as a sales leader and what you are looking to leave behind.

It is about getting those messages, whether it is an email or social media post, from a sales rep that you worked with who now owns their own company that is growing very quickly because of what you did. I have thousands of sales reps who send me messages, and many of them are my own sales reps who now own their own companies. Some of them are leading some of the biggest companies in the country, and I could not be prouder of them.

Some of them were chicken farmers, dishwashers, or the people who washed my truck. Now they are leading some of the biggest companies in the country, living a life they never thought was possible.

– **Chuck Thokey,** April 2026

Chapter 1

SALES LEADERSHIP 101

The most persistent problem that affects the majority of sales environments is the progressive inclination toward complacency.

Even inside the Top Rep community, we often use the playful contradiction of labeling sales reps as 'lazy' while also recognizing them as 'champions'. This intriguing paradox lies in the fact that many sales professionals tend to do just enough, or what they believe is sufficient, to close a deal. While others understand that if they do their job and go above and beyond a typical sales call, they are always at the top of the leaderboard and recognized as champions within their market.

This tendency is not limited to sales but reflects broader global trends. Whether you are looking for a service like getting your hair done or eating in a restaurant, providers often deliver the bare minimum to meet their obligations. Unfortunately, Sales is not immune to this trend.

Salespeople frequently enter the arena and execute only the chores necessary to secure business. What is the result? They become interchangeable commodities, and their offerings become indistinguishable from those of their competitors.

This discussion serves as the foundation of one of my presentations where I ask the audience if this scenario resonates with them. I then outline the necessary steps for sales success and conclude by asking them to raise their hands if it sounds familiar. Without fail, every hand in the room goes up.

In essence, you become a commodity, which implies that you have followed the same path as every other product or service in your category.

In this analogy, you are like a can of green beans on the shelf. The only difference is that one can cost more due to the presence of a big 'green giant' on the label, which means they have a higher marketing spend to promote that brand.

The biggest problems I often see in organizations stem from ineffective leadership and inadequate training. As the saying goes, 'Monkey see, monkey do'.

When new team members join, we place them in top performers' shadows with the directive to watch and learn. This is a habit that has continued since I first entered this industry, and unfortunately, many businesses, especially ones that are not mainly focused on sales, still behave in this manner. They support the 'watch and learn' philosophy.

This strategy has its drawbacks. When new team members shadow experienced colleagues or even business owners, they tend to pick up their mentor's bad habits rather than best practices. There is often no structured process or training regimen in place. Consequently, they settle for mediocre results.

The crux of the issue is that these team members don't realize what they don't know.

They feel they have received appropriate training, and if they have difficulty selling, they frequently blame it on excessive price. Unfortunately, in the world of commodities, and where they operate, the lowest price often prevails. Their pricing may be a problem, but it is just one piece of the larger puzzle. The root of the problem is a lack of comprehensive training and understanding of efficient sales strategies.

We know that we are in a value-based competition, and that is what sets us apart. This is why we can charge $5,000 - $10,000 more than our competitors and still secure the business. We do not just propose a product, an installation plan, and a price, we emphasize the value of what we offer.

Sales challenges often stem from various factors. One significant issue is assembling the right team. It is critical to have a team composed of individuals with the right sales acumen, rather than non-sales personnel.

Another problem is a lack of training and a clear understanding of how to deliver effective training. In addition, many companies struggle to integrate standardized procedures within their sales teams.

Furthermore, with the introduction of the Internet, the sales environment has been altered. Homeowners now conduct their own research, making them more informed consumers.

As sales representatives, if we embellish the truth or mislead in any way, the homeowner is quick to catch on. We've found that nearly half of all homeowners know what they want to buy before they talk to a salesperson. In many cases, all we have to do is not screw things up.

The extraordinary availability of information is a key obstacle in today's sales world. Homeowners and consumers in general want simpler and more educated answers to their problems. The most serious is that we are putting the wrong personnel into the field, equipped with the incorrect knowledge.

As we turn our focus to the sales staff, many key challenges emerge. First and foremost, it often begins with having the wrong people on the team. We frequently find ourselves with sales representatives who can merely 'fog a mirror', who are individuals who show signs of life but lack the necessary qualities for success.

Some sales leaders have the misconception that anyone can be trained to be successful in sales. However, my coaching experience, and many years in sales leadership has shown me that this is not the case.

Success in sales requires not just training but an innate drive and a genuine desire for success.

Sales leaders themselves play a key role in this context. Our observations reveal a distinct distribution pattern among them in the United States. Approximately 10% are excelling and thriving in their roles, while another 10% are considered 'effective'.

However, 60% of these leaders need coaching and training due to a lack of comprehensive understanding of what it takes to be a successful sales leader. Concerningly, 20% of this workforce should be replaced to facilitate constructive change and progress.

Another significant issue that we are dealing with is a lack of numerical comprehension. Many underperforming organizations prefer to keep the same sales crew for years without appropriate turnover or significant training initiatives.

While they may send their employees to conferences or seminars, there is frequently a need for more significant investment in training and development. As a result, these teams are somewhat stranded and unclear about their future actions.

Adding to the complexity is the lack of a standardized system or process. Each team member tends to have a unique approach to selling and communication. This absence of a structured system leads to inconsistencies in sales approaches. Allowing reps to stray too far from the system leads to restructured and lazy selling.

Another weakness that we notice is the inability to successfully finish negotiations. Some salesmen stress the position of 'sales consultant', providing advice on what customers need but are failing to ask for the purchase. They are unfamiliar with the closing process and frequently find themselves simply supplying information and leaving, hoping for a callback. Not being ready for what the prospect may say after price is given accounts for close rates under 40%.

This method leaves no space for follow-up, and many business owners believe that salespeople should handle this duty. This is typically an unreasonable expectation unless they have extraordinarily experienced and disciplined personnel on their teams, which is like looking for a unicorn.

Sales representatives are forward-thinking individuals who look for low-hanging fruit. However, when 18 out of 20 phone calls go to voicemail, they may feel their time is being wasted. To address this, dedicated follow-up personnel are often hired to ensure that follow-up tasks are completed efficiently, allowing sales representatives to focus on chasing new opportunities. This approach ensures a more efficient and effective sales process.

When I am brought in to assess a situation, my initial focus is on several key factors.

First and foremost, I scrutinize the sales leadership, as it sets the tone for the entire team. Next, I examine the sales team itself to understand the current dynamics and capabilities.

Another critical aspect that I consider is the type of opportunities available to the sales team. Do they have to actively prospect or sell door-to-door, or do they get most of their leads from outside sources? It is critical to understand the sales environment, and I have seen both scenarios in certain organizations that rely heavily on inbound leads.

These elements give me a solid platform to go into the existing procedures. However, the people component remains crucial in my evaluation since it is the foundation of every successful sales activity.

The fantasy we offer is one of long-term viability. When we evaluate a team and its leader, our primary aim is to have a long-term effect rather than to merely address current difficulties. It starts with educating the leader to successfully teach the staff and developing a culture of self-sufficiency.

If we only focus on teaching the staff and resolving difficulties without also empowering the management, problems tend to recur. This is because the leader frequently resorts to herding the team rather than successfully directing or leading it.

To achieve sustainability, we concentrate on training the sales leader. This involves imparting a clear understanding of their role, responsibilities, and expectations, as well as establishing mechanisms for accountability.

Then from there, we emphasize the importance of closely monitoring and analyzing sales metrics and understanding the dashboard. This means, holding the sales leader accountable every week. The reason for this is the natural deterioration process.

As soon as you take your vision or your focus off of what is needed, the deterioration process starts again. Ronald Reagan said it best when he said, "Trust, but verify."

Build the Machine

Few examples of business transformation are as amazing as my experience at O'Leary, a Pennsylvania-based company that went from less than $1 million in sales to a $6 million industry profit giant. They are now one of the most profitable roofing contractors in the United States.

What makes the O'Leary story unique is its transformation from a husband-and-wife partnership overseeing everything to a full-fledged company with a dedicated sales force and production team.

When we joined forces, the owner had been running the show single-handedly for over three decades. Together, we set out to build the company, gradually bringing in new personnel, including sales representatives, which in turn enabled them to expand the business. As a result, the owner was finally able to step back from the day-to-day operations and focus on strategically growing the company.

He often told me, "Chuck, I'll know I've succeeded when I can remove myself from the business."

He did achieve that milestone and today he oversees the company from a higher vantage point. He has increased his pricing to a level where his net profit margin well exceeds the typical 15-20%, which is a remarkable achievement in the industry.

The absence of people and defined processes was the primary issue we addressed in the O'Leary case. The owner initially handled everything himself, from lead generation to project management. This limited the company's expansion potential to what he could personally sell and install.

Our relationship with O'Leary underwent a strategic makeover. They started by establishing and training a sales staff, then progressively expanded efforts to encompass all other critical jobs. As a result, the organization is well-established and competently manned.

The initial part of our collaboration with O'Leary centered around the implementation of a comprehensive system. We could train staff to function within this framework once we had a system in place. This sales method is still an important part of O'Leary's business today.

Their growth was primarily facilitated by the systematic approach we introduced.

The owner's vision was not to become big, but to become highly efficient and profitable. He wanted to remove himself from the daily operations and witness the business running smoothly on its own. He wanted to build this 'machine', which we did, and he watched it run.

The machine now runs on its own.

It is generally easier to work with businesses that are a bit more established because we can make adjustments to their existing processes. Dealing with much smaller companies often means they have a limited budget, and it can be difficult to develop within those constraints.

If you find yourself in a scenario similar to O'Leary's, remember that it may never feel like the perfect time to develop, but it is always the right time to grow.

Start by finding that first person.

People often ask me how they can build a team. It all begins with one.

Once you have that first person on board, then you can start looking for the next one.

Instead of worrying about the total number of people you need, just focus on getting the next one.

Know the Numbers

When I entered a Cincinnati based organization, my initial purpose was to assist them in hiring a sales leader. However, recognizing the immediate potential, I decided to temporarily step into the role of the sales leader myself.

At the outset, the company established an ambitious target of generating $12 million to $14 million dollars in yearly sales. Surprisingly, we went from a $6-million-dollar pace to a $12-million-dollar reality in just six months.

This success can be attributed to our focus on numbers. Our intervention did not involve hiring more personnel, they already had a strong sales team in place.

The challenge lay in the team's lack of familiarity with their sales metrics. By analyzing these numbers and aligning them with organizational goals, we quickly attained our targets. This involved both training and elevating the performance of their second location. Instead of setting a five-year target to reach twelve million dollars, we achieved it within a mere six months.

Another challenge that we faced was office staff handling phone calls. To address this, we recognized the need for a dedicated phone team, given our $6 million revenue level.

In addition, we recognized the importance of having a dedicated sales contact for follow-up. We recognized that relying on sales reps to follow-up was ineffective, so we hired a specialist for this role. After appointments, this follow-up specialist took over, freeing the sales team to focus on new prospects.

The key to our quick expansion was putting the right people in the appropriate roles. People must understand that the emphasis is on people, then numbers, and ultimately the process.

We investigate to identify the real issues, just as we would in any other circumstance. While we hear the owner's point of view, our onsite presence reveals the root causes of their development slowdowns or failures. Often the root cause is a lack of understanding of their numbers. We prioritize team building to achieve specific goals over more advertising.

We make sure that we bring the team 'up'.

If I know I need ten people to achieve a particular goal, I proactively seek out those ten individuals. I then focus on mobilizing my marketing staff to support those ten people. I do not approach it by pushing the marketing staff and then figuring out how many people are required to handle the needs. Remember, you still have to onboard and train the new team members. This will give you more than enough time to get your marketing to the level needed to handle the added staff.

In this particular case, we established a dedicated phone room to handle leads and assessed the required number of leads. While we already had staff members, we did hire three additional people for the sales team. This is essentially how we facilitated growth.

The problem was that our office staff was answering the phones, and the sales team was struggling to close deals because they didn't have the information they needed, or they were not set up properly. We decided to bring in professionals whose job it was to manage appointments, so that the sales reps could focus on closing deals. Most companies foolishly rely heavily on the sales reps to run the entire selling process, then cross their fingers hoping they will actually close something.

This change resulted in an incredible outcome, including an additional $6 million in revenue, higher close rates, and increased team morale. It is important to recognize that using phone support has a ripple effect on the team, changing percentages and ratios. It has a positive impact on team cohesion, attitudes, and the team's ability to achieve their goals.

It all comes down to having the right people in the organization. If we want to expand, we need to make sure we are focusing our efforts on the right people.

A company's success depends on the caliber of its people.

Fire Them All

I went into an organization in Columbus, Ohio, where the business owner, despite being knowledgeable about numbers, admitted that he was a poor leader.

This admission alone spoke volumes about the state of his leadership. After examining his team dynamics, he realized that his team was running the show.

The staff mocked him, and laughter filled the air whenever initiatives needed to be implemented. We could not simply fix that situation, even though we were eager to do so.

If we had believed that training could be a solution, we would have pursued it. However, they were openly opposing everything he wanted and undermining his authority.

I gave him an unequivocal answer, "Fire them all."

He seemed frightened and desperate at first, then replied, "I was going to hire more people."

But I stood firm in my recommendations. "You can't add to a company that has a mutiny going on inside it."

I told him. "They have no respect for you, so if you want to start over, let's do it."

This is exactly what we did.

We assessed the business owner's weaknesses. It became clear that running a team was one of his shortcomings, but we still needed someone to oversee the entire company or team.

He followed my advice and began searching for an integrator, someone willing to do what he could not. This person would be responsible for training, holding others accountable, and implementing strategies needed to move the company forward.

Next, he took the critical step of recruiting an entirely new staff, including office staff, sales personnel, and production staff.

We worked closely together throughout the process. His new integrator spearheaded the recruiting effort, while we provided the necessary support and guidance while holding them accountable.

We applied pressure when progress seemed to stall. We had to do this because the business owner did not like to be pressured.

Nothing beats a solid deadline for motivation. We set deadlines for filling specific positions, and I sought their commitment. I would categorically ask them, "Can you do it? Is this going to be done, or are we going to come up with a bunch of excuses by the time we hit that date? This has a deadline."

I emphasized that deadlines have a purpose, and their commitment plays a huge part. While I knew I could assemble a complete sales team in two weeks, I challenged them to do it within two months because there were other priorities as well.

By creating a new team, we ensured that each member was genuinely interested in the company's success. These new team members were motivated to support the owner's success while achieving their own.

The goal was not just to replace current employees, but to create an entirely new organization.

We established a thorough training structure to prepare new employees. There was an organized training program for salespeople, and the same was true for administrative functions. We established specific standard operating procedures for each role so that new hires knew exactly what was expected of them and there was no room for guessing.

This situation highlights a crucial principle: a company's fate hinges on its staff. In this case, the staff transformation breathed life into the business, saving it from its previous decline.

As a result, revenue tripled, despite there being little initial revenue. This company is now one of the fastest-growing companies in Columbus.

Make Up for Your Weaknesses

In the corporate world, I have repeatedly come across the story of organizations on the verge of disaster, held back by a succession of errors and misfortunes, who then find the courage to make a simple decision that changes everything.

Surprisingly, we often see a recurring theme among failing leaders and owners: a lack of someone to help them in the areas where they struggle.

The solution is to hire someone to compensate for your weaknesses until you can fix them.

One company that I worked with had previously failed four times in the same industry. Their lifeline came in the form of a family member recognizing this company's need for intervention.

The transformation that followed was nothing short of remarkable, with the company rising to become the largest dealer of acrylic baths in the area.

The owner was a competent businessperson but struggled with management.

My first order of business upon arrival was to replace the current sales rep. They had a know-it-all attitude and refused to listen. When I connect with a sales team and get comments like, "Yes, I know", "Yes, we do that", or "Yes, that's what we do", it is a dead giveaway that they are not open to change, and I am not going to waste any more time with them.

When I encounter a team that says, "Chuck, we are open to doing things differently, adjusting our approach, or changing our communication," it is like a breath of fresh air. It's time to get to work.

In these situations, I am eager to roll up my sleeves and get started. I look at whether they are a good fit for the company over time because there are a lot of people I like who are not a good fit. They are not able to sell because it is just not in their DNA. The company's culture is built by the people you bring into the organization. Unfortunately, it's also built by those you tolerate bad behavior from.

But in the case of this company, in order to facilitate their progress, we initiated the development of a sales system, a training program, and efficient processes within the organization. At the same time, we started hiring for the new sales staff.

This approach transformed the organization, which started as a small company with one of the smallest territories and has since expanded to three locations, including the two largest cities in their state.

Their growth continues because they now understand what it takes to be successful. The principle at play here is the trifecta of: people, training, and processes.

While the owner had a firm grasp of the numbers, it was the alignment of these three factors that propelled the organization forward.

Previously, he was relatively unknown within the franchise; even his supplier would not give him the time of day. Today, his name is recognized by everyone. His vendors are actively seeking his opinion. They are willing to work together and even provide rewards such as sports tickets and trips. They have finally recognized him as a legitimate contender, and someone worth watching in the profession. Best of all, he is moving quickly to the top of the bath franchise leaderboard.

That Small Piece

I was asked to work with a company in Mississippi that was so well-established and well-managed, I felt I would be able to learn from them.

At the same time, they had identified a specific pain point that was crying out for a solution. The company struggled with follow-up and a few other small areas within the front of the business, which surprised me.

I have found that no two challenges are ever the same. When I step into a new company, people ask me, "Can't you just give us access to your videos?"

I tell them, "Yeah, but that's not going to help you. We have to come in and find out what's wrong."

There is no one-size-fits-all answer. Every company needs a personalized strategy that gets to the heart of their problems.

A rigorous follow-up strategy was created in Tennessee, with a dedicated office staff member supervising the CRM system. This included data cleansing, seamless task development, preventing salespeople from dropping the ball, and responding to client queries as soon as possible. A new leader was brought in and training was offered, which resulted in enhanced success, particularly in the function of sales leader. Despite early opposition, the new leader was able to effectively handle the situation.

Earning respect is not about making sales reps blindly follow orders. It is more about how a leader can positively impact the organization to empower sales reps to achieve greater success. This involves various aspects, including training and implementing competitions.

Recently, I worked with a leader on expressing passion during sales meetings, even if it meant getting a bit intense at times. Sometimes, that is necessary to motivate the team. We just made a small change, but the change that took place was a big piece of it. It was the grease that enabled it to happen.

The existing team had the potential. Our role was to provide the tools and guidance needed to unlock that potential. It is all centered around a sales leader's ability to connect with and understand their team because, ultimately, again, it all boils down to the people.

Making Hard Decisions

In this line of work, you have to make challenging decisions and have tough conversations.

I recall a painful case in which the sensitive dynamics of the family were intertwined with their company, resulting in a difficult decision. It is a regular scenario in our sector, where family connections frequently come to the fore and expectations collide with reality.

As a result, I had to advise a business owner to fire his son. When he hesitated, I advised him to then just go ahead and provide his son with a comfy La-Z-Boy chair, and ask him to sit in the corner.

This kind of situation is a regular occurrence in the home renovation sector, where family relations frequently play a role. Often, the son owns the firm, while the father works as the sales leader or in a sales role.

In some instances, the roles are reversed, with the father as the owner and the son in a leadership role simply because he is family. However, being a great salesperson does not necessarily translate into being a good leader. We have to tell them that if they are bringing someone into management, they must be prepared to let them go if they don't perform.

If you cannot imagine firing a family member, whether it would be your mother, father, sister, cousin, or brother, they should not be in that position. Let's assume you discover the next day that putting them in that situation was a bad idea. Are you willing to put up with it? This occurs frequently. The answer I typically get is yes, but their actions speak differently when that situation comes up, and it will.

Despite early expectations, it is sometimes clear that the family member option was not the best one. In such instances, it is critical to be willing to make difficult decisions for the benefit of the company's growth.

In this case, my client had to fire his son because his son was very combative and not willing to put in the work. He had an easy upbringing and even though he wanted his son to grow in the organization, he simply was not good for the role. He was not a good fit for the team.

The son performed poorly in sales, but they were considering putting him in a leadership role anyway. I told them, "Your organization can grow, and you have all the necessary training in place.

However, the reason your organization is not growing is because your son is hindering its growth. He is content with his current income, and he is lazy."

As a result, they were stagnating and facing several issues within the sales team, including favoritism. When we begin to assess the situation, I always start with the sales leader. In this case, it was clear that the current sales leader was not the right fit. He showed up late for our meeting, slouched in his chair, and was more interested in his phone than in our conversation. It was clear that he was not taking the role seriously, and that made the decision easy.

When I returned to the father with my assessment, I told him, "You may not like what I have to say, and it is up to you whether you act on it, but the problem within your organization is indeed your son. He lacks the discipline for the position, and he has no intention of listening to my advice."

The father's response was, "I know."

Even with that acknowledgment, I couldn't help but ask, "Did you need to pay me to come in and tell you what you already knew?"

His answer was, "No, I just want you to tell me what to do from here."

As a result, we had to find a new function for his son, who eventually opted to resign rather than accept a demotion because his pals were his sales team.

We subsequently hired a new sales leader, which fixed the majority of the difficulties. We did, however, have certain members of the sales staff that decided to leave because their protector wasn't there any longer. The acceptance of lazy behavior came to an abrupt end.

This concept emphasizes the need to hire the proper sales leader. While family-run companies are widespread, it is critical to check that the family members you bring on board are truly competent in carrying out their responsibilities. The father saw that his son was the source of the problem, but he was unwilling to confront it. Finally, I had to intervene and make the difficult choice to let go of his son, saving the father from having to do it himself.

You can address almost any sales-related problem.

Addressing these difficulties successfully is the primary idea underlying our training and the training of any company.

In today's landscape, homeowners are more informed than ever, and it is crucial to understand their perspective. Instead of the traditional approach of 'park and puke', where we simply present information, we now focus on asking questions.

When selling, I start by acknowledging that the homeowner has likely researched their project online. I ask if they would be willing to share any images or ideas that they have found to tailor our discussion to their preferences and needs.

It is quite common to witness a flood of pictures from homeowners when discussing their preferences. However, instead of immediately discussing what I want to sell, I focus on what they envision for their bathroom.

Even if I cannot use every detail from such images due to franchise restrictions, I select components that correspond to their aspirations.

For example, if they prefer the aesthetic of marble or a frameless door, I will stress such features. This method permits me to comprehend their viewpoint before giving my expertise.

Before I tell you what I know, I am going to find out what you know.

The solution to this challenge lies in asking questions, which reminds me of the old game of 'Battleship'. I inquire to uncover what is on the opponent's 'board', just as a Battleship player fires questions into the unknown, trying to locate what is hidden.

I ask the potential customer questions because I do not assume that they know exactly what they need. And just because I know what the last ten customers needed does not mean that the next one will have the same needs.

The same logic applies to helping sales leaders. I ask them a series of questions to assess their expertise.

Once I have that information, I can tailor my advice accordingly. I do not want to talk to them and get answers like, "I already know that," or "I've done this training before."

Similarly, when working with a sales leader in charge of a sales team, it is critical to identify the team's challenges. I teach them how to ask these questions of their teammates and occasionally of themselves.

However, before we can intervene, individuals must demonstrate their willingness to commit to the necessary steps. Before we decide to do anything, I need to know that you are willing to do what we want you to do.

Do you want to start a recreational league or a professional team?

This analogy provides a valuable insight. When you are engaged in sports, are you part of a recreational league where everyone gets a turn, or are you striving to be on a professional team where you have to earn your spot and continually prove your worth? This principle extends up to the coach or sales leader.

In a professional team, each member must perform at their best, and the coach or, in this case, the sales leader, has to ensure this. They cannot step onto the field and play the game themselves. Instead, they must guide and lead from the sidelines. The key is to select the right players and train them effectively to achieve victory.

Again, are you steering a recreational league or a professional team?

This may be a difficult decision for business owners, especially when they discover their organization resembles a group of whining and moaning youngsters on a 'Little League' team who did not get their turn at bat.

Sales are not equitable, and there is nothing fair about sales.

Everything you make in sales is yours to keep. Nothing is handed to you.

When people complain that others get more leads, I tell them to look at their figures to find out why.

Sales is all about what you have done recently, not what you established last month.

Yesterday's accomplishments are no longer news.

Chapter 2

DO YOU HAVE WHAT IT TAKES?

When I ask people why they want to be a sales leader, they tell me about their tenure and feel as though they deserve the position since they have been in the industry for a long time.

Okay, that's fine. But being put into a sales leadership position is not about how long you have worked, but about why you want the position. Can you lead the team at a high level without thinking about your own paycheck?

In most cases, what we find is that people want to be sales leaders for all the wrong reasons, like being able to pick their own schedule. Instead, the 'right' reason for wanting to be a sales leader should be something like 'helping others achieve dreams that they never thought they could achieve.'

When I was in the mortgage industry, I was one of the highest-producing mortgage agents in the country.

I had the opportunity to help a lady named Tanya who was about to quit, and I showed her how to be successful. When I was finished helping her and several others, I realized that I had gotten more joy out of that than I did closing all day long.

Even though I made incredible money, I loved the satisfaction that I got from helping the others have the success I had achieved. As of today, she is one of the top closing professionals when it comes to finance & mortgage.

In fact, she is on the speaking circuit now, and back then, she had been thinking about going back to being an executive assistant before I helped her.

I have helped so many sales reps who are now sales leaders. One man that I worked closely with as a sales professional is one of the highest-ranking positions inside of EOS and is very well known in that space.

I have a big EOS integrator, and they said, "Let me tell you about EOS." I asked him, "Have you heard of Barry Barrett?" His eyes got wide, and he said that everyone within EOS knows Barry Barrett.

I'm proud that Barry used to be one of my sales reps.

The reason for wanting to be a sales leader is not going to be the same for everyone, but the main reason should be that they truly want to help people out, that they feel that they have something inside of them that they can manage, and that they can lead people the right way.

Even in results-based leadership, where we are servant leaders, we grease the gears. Our sales reps don't see that they are actually above us, and our job is to give them everything that they need.

We give them the training, we give them the tools, we give them the technology, and we are there to support them so that they can be successful. We also lead them in a way that we can hold them accountable.

When I was speaking in Pittsburgh, someone told me, "Man, you are so aggressive on stage, and you speak in such a strong way." I must make an impact on the audience if they are to take action on anything they pick up at the event.

The reason that I do this is because I want them to know that if they are going to promote their top rep because they feel like they can clone the top rep, all they are doing is taking a stallion out of the race and putting them into the stables.

This doesn't mean that putting a top rep into that position cannot be good, but you better make sure that they are being put into that position for all the right reasons.

Are they uncoachable? There are a lot of sales leaders that are uncoachable, they may be know-it-alls, or feel as though they have something to prove. When I am talking to a new sales leader, I poke the bear the whole time I am talking to them. I am waiting for them to be defensive, and as soon as they are defensive, I will point it out and say, "Hey, this may not be for you. If me poking you makes you mad, this may not be for you. Whether you agree with it or not, you should be able to take constructive criticism in stride. If you are going to be defensive, we can't work together."

If I accuse you of certain things or if I give you criticism, is this criticism something you are willing to take on the chin, whether you agree with it or not, or are you going to come back at me with a lot of defensiveness?

Are you going to tell me that you do all that, or that you know all that? If yes, then you are not meant to be a sales leader. When someone is there to help you, soak in the knowledge even if some of it is a refresher of what you already know.

Another thing that will stop you from being a sales leader is being undisciplined and unaccountable. Undisciplined means that we cannot even hold you accountable to what it is that you are supposed to do, so how can we expect that you are going to hold your sales reps accountable to what they are expected to do?

You also need to be engaging with your team. A lot of these sales managers are boring, and when they go into these sales meetings, they just don't know what to do. They can't engage their team, and they can't be fun. You need to engage your team in what they are supposed to do, and what they are supposed to learn.

About 20% of people I talk to who want to be sales leaders are cut out for the job.

10% of them are rock stars. When I see them, I think, 'This guy or gal has it going on. They know what they're doing.' Another 10% are just effective, like putting in a hall monitor. They just keep everyone moving in the right direction, but other than that, they have no idea what they are doing.

60% of them are desperate for coaching and training and have no idea what they are doing. They are usually either very new, or they have never had a mentor in that arena. The last 20% just need to be replaced right off the bat.

The keys to sales leadership are knowing your numbers, making the expectations clear, being able to understand forecasting, forecasting their numbers, managing the activity and not the results, managing the sales calendar like a pro, having engaging sales meetings, extreme discipline and accountability, and understanding recruiting, training, and onboarding.

Do you have what it takes?

Are You Coachable?

Behind that curtain, we are going to come at you, the owner is going to come at you, the sales reps are going to come at you, and they are going to give you certain criticism. They are going to accuse you of certain things, and say that you know or don't know certain things.

If I were to come at you with constructive criticism, would you be willing to take that criticism, whether you feel you know it well or you feel like you could do better in certain areas? Is this skill something that you would be willing to learn?

I said it already, but I'm going to say it again. Anytime you feel like you are going to tell me that you know this, or that you already know everything there is to know about sales management, you have already lost. You have no business being in this industry because as a sales leader, you are always going to continue to learn.

The moment that you start blocking and saying, 'Oh, I already know that', or 'I'm already good at that', you need to go back to sales, or do something else.

If I were to teach you about your schedule, and you were to tell me that you already know how to deal with your schedule, and maybe you do, but there are certain things that you can learn about understanding your sales schedule, you need to keep your mouth shut and learn.

People look at me and say, "Chuck, you don't talk much."

The reason why I don't talk much is because I would rather learn more than give information. If I am speaking with someone who I don't need to teach and would rather learn from, I am going to keep my mouth shut and learn as much as I can.

There are a lot of things that come up that I have done before, but then all of a sudden something comes that I have never heard of before.

As a sales leader, this is hard to do because we feel like our ego is being challenged, and we feel like the knowledge and the reason why we are a sales leader is being challenged.

This is no different from being a sales trainer, where when a new sales trainer comes along, you want to feel like you are the best in the industry. It is hard to keep your mouth shut and your brain open, because you want to feel like you are better than the person who is speaking.

If you were that good, then you would keep your mouth shut and listen, because there is something that will be said that you are going to want to take notes on.

I have grown to where I am in this industry because I am willing to continue to learn, and I am not so egotistical to think that I know everything, because I don't.

As a sales leader, you should never know everything or feel like you know everything. You should feel like you know your job, but you should never truly feel like you know everything.

This is very hard for a lot of people and disqualifies sales leaders faster than anything else.

I have called many owners and let them know that I could not work with their sales manager, because they are not listening. They just want to tell me how much they know, and not listen to what's being discussed.

I have worked with many owners whom I have told that I could not work with them, as owners, because I knew they weren't listening.

You have to know that someone who is good at coaching and training starts from number one or number zero and works their way up. They know that you may be excellent at something, but they cannot just come in at a higher level, assuming that you know everything below that level.

Someone who is coachable is willing to shut their mouth, open their mind, and fill the gaps.

You may not know it, but there are always gaps in teaching your sales reps how to close. You may know how to close, but I may say something inside, or you might hear something from someone else that will fill a gap that you didn't even know you had.

I will go to conventions to speak, and then all of a sudden find myself grabbing my phone because I just heard something from another speaker that I had never heard before. I am willing to shut up and open my mind because I know that I am coachable.

Someone who is coachable is willing to fill the gaps and willing to learn from others. No matter what that skill may be, they are always willing to take it in.

They will be less likely to show their ego by opening their mouth and telling someone all that they know; no one cares.

If someone is teaching you, and you can't wait to speak up and show everyone how much you know, that is a problem. Shut up and listen!

Are You Disciplined and Accountable?

You need to be very disciplined with your schedule, punctuality, and responsibilities.

You have to hold yourself accountable and be disciplined enough to get everything done, especially when it comes to holding sales meetings. 'The speed of the leader is the speed of the gang' is a good way of explaining this.

It is very important to know if they are disciplined enough to check their numbers, or if they are disciplined enough to always know what is going on with their sales reps and listen to their calls, or if they are disciplined enough to put themselves on the calendar to ride with a sales rep so many times in a month.

If you can't be disciplined or held accountable, you cannot hold your sales reps accountable and make sure that they are disciplined enough to do what they need to do each day to be successful.

It is so easy to not do the most important things because the most important things take work. It takes you out of the office, and it is not as fun as sitting and watching YouTube all day long.

When you are reading a book, be disciplined enough to highlight the things that you can use from that book, and be disciplined enough to use them.

This is a huge problem, and it is getting worse. The reason is because we are less disciplined and accountable as a society.

Everyone is so ingrained in their apps and can sit on TikTok for hours on end. People spend more time talking about what they see on social media than what they did today.

If you ask someone what they have accomplished, they are more apt to tell you all about what they saw on social media.

We are less disciplined and less accountable than we ever were, just because there are so many more things that are taking our attention away from what we actually should be doing.

The sales leader needs to be accountable to their sales reps rather than the company.

Remember that we are servant leaders. We want to make sure that they have everything that they need, and part of that is knowledge.

We need to be held accountable for everything that we are holding them accountable for.

They also need to be disciplined to be ready for the day.

Sales leaders often come into their day wondering what they are going to do, and that is another problem.

If they are disciplined, the last thing they do today is to lay out what they are going to do tomorrow.

People are not generally good about doing that, and most sales leaders do not even know they are supposed to be doing that.

Sales reps should know what appointments they are going to or where they should prospect.

Success depends on the sales rep knowing what they are going to do the next day and where they are going to do it.

If it is a phone rep, they should know where they are going to find the people that they are going to call. Is this a bucket of phone numbers or prospects in their CRM that is given to them? They need to know where the list is going to come from.

In a phone room, they are disciplined enough to dial the next number or to keep dialing so that they can hit so many dials an hour and so many leads in a day.

This is the same thing with the canvass team. How many knocks can they get in an hour? How many leads can they get in an hour? They all need to be held accountable, but they need to be disciplined enough to stay focused.

In fact, I would say, discipline translates to focus.

As a society, we are pulled in so many different directions. If you ever work from home, do you feel that you are less focused at home than you are working in an office?

At home, you think of 20 other things that you are supposed to do other than your job, in many cases.

As a society, we are undisciplined because we have so many things that we would rather be doing or feel we should be doing than what we really should be focused on.

As a sales leader, it's important that we stay proactive and spend less time being reactive. If you find yourself being reactive a majority of the time, it's a direct reflection on your leadership. We train your team to perform in a certain way so that we are successful and have less issues to deal with. Being a hero and firefighter all the time does not make you a more valuable leader. It shows how disorganized you are. Staying one step ahead of the owner and the team takes work and focus.

Are You Willing to Take a Call at Dinner?

Sales leaders want to be sales leaders because they think they get to leave at five, but that is not the case.

You might get to leave the office at five, but if that phone rings, and it is a sales rep, they could be needing help.

You never know why that sales rep is calling, but you should always look at it as if they are in-house. They are on an appointment, and they need me, so it doesn't matter what I am doing. This could be during a sporting event, if I jump up and head to the exit, even my daughter knows that a sales rep just called me. She knows it so well because she has seen it so many times.

If a sales rep is on the line, I am going to go, and I will be right back. It could happen even when I am at an anniversary dinner with my wife.

People look at that and think it is just insane. They say, "You are going to get out of an anniversary date with your wife, just to take a call?"

Yes, because my sales rep may be in a house needing help to close a job.

I tell the sales reps, "Guys if you are going to call me when I am taking my wife out to dinner tonight for our anniversary, it better be good. If you are in-house, then call me, but don't call because you just want to celebrate something. This is not the night for that."

I let my sales reps know that, and if they do call, that means that they are in-house and need concessions. They need me to help close a deal or something, and so I will get up in the middle of that dinner.

This is why sales managers may question if this job is right for them if that is what they have to do. I will take phone calls up to midnight.

Sales reps may be in an eight o'clock appointment, but this may be a four-hour meeting that should have only been two hours. If the homeowner is going back and forth, it can easily be a four-hour meeting. It is midnight, and they are still in the customer's house.

When sales leaders think that their days are done at five, that is not the case.

Sales leaders will often work before everyone gets into the office and till the wee hours of the night. They are held accountable for the success of that team, and they are the lifeline for that team.

When people ask, "Who do I call when something happens?" I don't care what that something is, you call the sales leader. There may be some technical questions, then you can call the production manager, but most of the time, it is the sales leader.

A sales rep who would want a promotion may not see that part of the sales manager role. Even when they are the ones calling, they don't recognize the fact that they just took that sales leader out of dinner.

We don't say, "Hey, man, I'm in the middle of dinner. What have you got?" I am not going to make them feel bad for calling me.

They don't see that I have 26 sales reps. This one sales rep may have only called me once in three months, but he doesn't understand that the others call me all the time.

Since they don't see that, they may think that the sales leader doesn't do anything. They think that he just sits in his office, and occasionally, he gets out and rides with us, or he has a meeting once a week.

They don't see that there are three meetings today to be held accountable to the rest of the company. I have a marketing meeting, and I have a meeting with the owner or the president because they are not happy with my performance or the performance of the team. I may have to give a report to the board. Whatever the case may be, they don't see that.

The sales leaders are always in meetings, being held accountable to make sure that the other departments have a reason to run.

If it wasn't for sales, we would not need marketing.

If it wasn't for sales, we would not need the phone room.

If it wasn't for sales, we would not need production.

If you are in those departments, don't worry, if it weren't for you, sales wouldn't be needed. It's truly a team effort.

I am held accountable for all of that, and I have to give reports of what we are doing.

We are booking all of these appointments, and they are coming back to us saying that we are not doing our job, and asking if we can close a little bit harder.

We are held accountable for everyone, but only the sales leader sees that.

Sales Meetings: Are You Able to Engage Your Team?

A lot of sales leaders are insanely boring people.

When they look at a sales meeting, they have never experienced a very well-run sales or motivational meeting.

Alternatively, the way that I like to talk about sales meetings is that you have two hours to affect the success of the next seven days.

There are two types of meetings that we have as sales leaders.

We have sales meetings that should be about two hours long, and then we have 'power hour', which should be every morning to go over the appointments with the team of what happened the previous day.

When reps are finished with their appointment, there is one more piece of accountability because now they have to report what happened in that appointment the next morning.

If I ask them, "What happened with this person? How did that go?," they have to go through exactly what happened, and they cannot use excuses, because they are going to be called out on it.

We make this positive, the team works together to correct the activities that happened the day prior. Allow the team to discuss certain appointments and what should have happened. Call out different reps and ask what they would have done if they were in the house. I say this again, this is to be a positive experience for the reps. This should be the start to their day and you need to make a positive and motivational impact.

The team wants to work 'with' you or 'for' you. If they look at you as just a pawn or somebody that they have to report to, the respect won't be there.

You want your people to look at you and say, "He affected my life. He affects the way that I live life. I find him motivational. They have my best interest in mind. They truly care what happens with my growth in this company."

They want to look at you as a mentor and a sales leader should be looked at as a mentor to their people. When those people leave or that sales manager moves on, they can look back and say, "My favorite sales manager was Chuck because he wasn't always nice. He always told me I was accountable for what I was supposed to do. I never liked it at the time, but I am a better person because of it. He taught me how to be the best. He made me more successful and more money than I ever thought I could."

If you are not engaging with your people, they will never say any of that.

The other part of this is that engaging means that a two-hour sales meeting feels like ten minutes, that they are having fun, and that they learn a lot. We don't call people out in sales meetings, and you cannot be engaging by ridiculing people. This has to be a positive experience.

We have to make an impact in every meeting, but sometimes we have to show our passion, which is a code for me being an asshole, but I have to show my passion when I get upset in a meeting. This may be once or twice a year, when I have to get upset in a meeting because of the performance of the team. I was concerned to put this in the book because it's not always understood. You can get passionate in a meeting and control the narrative at the same time. Have a predetermined point you are trying to drive into them and control yourself during this time. If you can't control your frustration, this is not for you.

Sometimes we are not doing what we are supposed to be doing, or we are not performing the way we are supposed to be performing. We are getting beaten by the market or other companies in the market because we are not doing what we are supposed to be doing.

This passion has to be pre-planned; you can never get upset in a meeting without having it planned out. Just like an argument that you have with your spouse, if you do not pre-plan, you are going to end up saying things you wish you didn't say. You will say things that you mean, but you just didn't mean to say.

When you engage your team, you are making an impact. You are going to make an impact in many different ways, and it has to be looked at as positive in the end. Even when I am going to get passionate in a sales meeting, I will round it off, at the end, very positively.

I am going to let them know in the end, "Guys, I love each one of you. I think you are the best at what we do in the industry. We can just do it better, and I know you guys have it in you. I don't know why we just happened to get a little bit lazy over the last couple of weeks, but I know you can do it better. If any of you feel that you have some personal issues going on, that you feel that that is why your performance is affected, please come and see me. This is not the time to bring that up. If you got in a fight with your wife or somebody is going through other serious personal issues, come see me outside the meeting. I will take you out to eat, we will go out for drinks, or whatever. Do not let it go past this meeting, and do not let it go past this day. This is the last day of our downward spiral, and we are going back in the other direction."

We have to make that impact with them, and the engagement is inside what we do. Sometimes engagement is doing something other than sales that day, and saying, "Guys, we are shutting this day down. We are going to play golf. One way or another, as a team, we are going to blow off some steam, and we are going to go have some fun." It's time for a reset.

There are a lot of different ways that we can engage, but you have to engage the team because of the impact that engagement has on the team means they see the team leader as someone they want to work with. They feel like you have their best interest in mind.

Are You Willing to Make Less Money?

This comes as a surprise to a lot of sales leaders. You need to be prepared not to be the highest paid member of your team.

They ask, "Well, don't we get overrides?" Yeah, you get overrides. There is no doubt that you get overrides, but if you look at the top performing sales reps, the sales leaders should rarely make more than the top half of the sales team. The sales leaders are getting paid too much at that point.

There are very few situations where the sales leader should be out selling because if they are selling, they are not leading. I know that some people look at this as leading by example. If you plan on selling, you better have someone who is learning from you riding along.

Maybe the reason why you are selling is because someone called in sick, and you don't have another rep to send out, and then you can pick up the deal.

Sales leaders should not be out constantly running appointments. The sales reps will not look at that as, 'Wow, he's really good', instead they are going to look at that as, 'Damn, they are stealing more opportunities from us. He is only selling because he is cherry-picking his leads'.

The reason why they are a sales leader and the reason why I was a sales leader is that I put more value on the lives that I changed, lives that I affected, the families that I affected, and the livelihoods of those families, than I did on my paycheck.

If your focus is money, stop, and stay at a sales rep position. Your stress level of being a sales rep will be so much less than as a sales manager. You will make less and your stress will be through the roof, and if it is not, then you are not working hard enough.

Most sales reps do not see that, and they think that sales managers make too much, and they don't do anything. In many cases they are right.

Many sales leaders are in it for all the wrong reasons.

If you are in it for all the right reasons, it is because you are in it to change lives, and you are in it to affect the bottom line. You might find out that you are excellent at sales, but you are even better at producing sales champions, and you feel as though it is your calling.

Ultimately, we affect lives, we change lives, we give people a life that they never thought they could have, and we take people who never thought they could make a certain living and make that a reality for them. If this is not at the top of your list, then leadership is not right for you.

Do we make good money? Yes.

Do we have good livelihoods? Yes.

Do we enjoy our job? Absolutely.

But the most important part of our job is that we want to change lives.

Chapter 3

RECRUITING: DRAFTING YOUR PLAYERS

To be successful, it is important that a good sales leader pick a great team.

When a sales leader is able to hand-pick each person, they will then be responsible for the actions of the team that they chose.

So, how do you go about drafting your players?

First, you have to define the sales culture. When you are interviewing, you have to know what you are interviewing for, find your sales reps, and assess them so that you know their skills.

There are different ways of interviewing and different things that we are looking for in those interviews. When I interview a sales rep, it is more of what I am looking for, rather than what they say.

It is also understanding a 'strong bench'. How many reps do I need to have a strong bench of players?

We need to look at this as a team, and if we look at this as a brand-new sports team, the way that the hierarchy may fall may not be the same as it was previously.

The previous sales leader or owner may have had favorites that they played. Now, with this new sales leader coming in, he doesn't know these people, and he hasn't worked with them before. Now he gets the opportunity to put them in a place on a hierarchy based on the skill that they see.

It is important that when you join a new team, you don't just start nixing people. You might start bringing other people on, but give the people that are there anywhere between three and six months. Unless it's completely obvious that they have been there too long and the previous leader was just too weak to let them go.

Give them that opportunity to buy into you, to buy into your philosophy on sales and how you manage, and then decide whether they are a right fit for your team.

When a business is not performing, an owner will often want to bring in a new sales leader. If that leader is smart, they will quickly see that the company brought them in to try to fix something that was broken.

They may find out that the company's sales reps are worn out, so they don't want to do anything extra or more than what they need to do. Along those same lines, they are not going to go outside their job description to make a sale.

They may say, "We've always been able to just say that we don't want to go and visit with somebody in a trailer," or "I called early because it was an hour away." Well, that is going to change.

If a sales rep shows laziness, they may be let go and have the chance to be successful somewhere else. If they were allowed to be lazy in that organization, it would be very hard to get them to perform unless they feel it's time for them to change.

The easiest solution, when you have a group of lazy individuals, is to give them the shot and see if they rise to the occasion, but you have to lay it out for them. Let them know that, 'Yeah, folks, we are going to work here. What was ok before will not be accepted any longer.'

Put what is expected of them in writing, so that they will see what they need to do.

This is where, in our work, we help sales leaders determine categories with a 'sales rep matrix', which will help determine if sales reps need to be coached and trained, or if they have a very bad attitude, and not much skill, whether it be skill of the product or skill in selling. In that case, they need to be let go, and that should be an easy decision. Based on the matrix, do we need to isolate them, or are they rock stars?

I have had several organizations that I have walked into where there were rock stars. These guys are excellent, and they are always willing to jump in and help out, anywhere that is needed.

But long story short, we need to look at a sales rep's attitude, and their attitude can be a wide range of things. Their attitude is based on their willingness to help others, their attitude in the office, and how they treat others. Are they positive in the meetings and agreeable to change that needs to happen within the organization?

What is their skill level? We need to look at their skill level for sales, and their skill level for the products and services themselves. Do they close at a high rate and are they profitable? Does the customer enjoy working with them and the information they are given? Are they willing to share that knowledge with the rest of the team?

If they have a great attitude, but their skills are just lacking a little bit, then we decide that maybe they just need to be coached and trained. If they are rock stars, then we just need to make sure that we don't put them on a pedestal.

When sales leaders start to use this matrix, it becomes something that they can't put down. I use it quarterly with my own sales team.

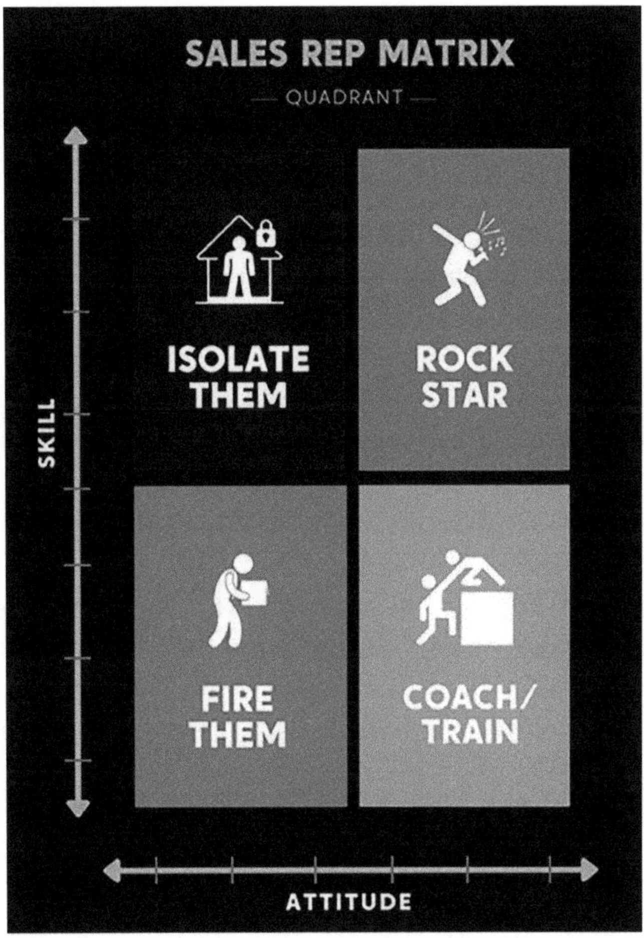

When I work with a sales leader and I ask them, "Tell me about this person and tell me about that person," we are going to write down what they are good at, and what they need help with. When we see what they need help with, those are their gaps.

Maybe they have a confidence issue, it could be anything. Now we will know what you need when it comes to coaching and training. Will they get into that rock star status? We don't know. It is not that they can't stay if they can't get there, as long as their performance is at acceptable levels. We will know what needs to be coached and trained.

When we look at the rock star status, it is not just because they have high sales numbers, it is because they work very well with others. They answer questions in the sales meetings or the group text, and they help other sales reps. They don't act selfishly, or keep all the information to themselves. If someone asks, "Hey, how did you do that?" If the answer is, "Well, I'm not going to share that with you," that is not a rock star.

We also have to be very careful with rock stars that we do not put them on a pedestal and say, "We couldn't do this without you. We would never be where we are today if it weren't for you." They will never learn anything else because we told them that they don't need to learn anything else. We show appreciation and give them a lot of love, but we need to watch what we say. Before you know it, they will hold it over your head, and say, "I need to be paid more. Like you said, you can't do this without me." Reps will either be put on the pedestal by a manager or owner, or they will put themselves there after a few good months or a year. Reps that take that step onto the pedestal will eventually exit the industry or simply be so hard to work with that they simply aren't worth keeping, it doesn't matter how much they produce for the company.

The next one is easy. If they have a bad attitude, and they are just very low on the skill set side, it is very easy. Fire them. Even if they are new, if they have a bad attitude, they're gone.

There are times when you earn the right to have a character flaw, but the period when you are new isn't that time. If you have been there a while, and you have put up some numbers, and maybe your attitude goes in the toilet for a little bit, it is okay. A lot of times it is personal issues that bring it out, maybe they just need to blow off some steam. I will give them a 'temporary' pass, but if they are brand new and that happens, it is time to go.

Then we can look at someone who has a lot of skill, and their clients love them, but no one in the office can stand them. You can see that they are just a very negative person, and always want to complain about the leads. "Hey, I saw that you gave Tim this lead. I should have had that lead! I'm the one at the top of the leaderboard! I should have had that lead!" When they say that in the middle of the sales meeting, we need to consider isolating them. It used to be that they were considered toxic, so we just have to get rid of them. You have a delicate decision to make due to the culture issues in keeping them. Do you feel they can turn their attitude around or is this a character flaw.

I am not going to take a good closer, where the clients love them, and send them to our competitor. If you decide to isolate them, let them know, "Hey, we don't want you in any of the sales meetings. We don't want you talking to any of the salespeople. We don't want you talking to anybody in the office. You're going to deal strictly with me." You will want to coach them through this time so they understand what they need to do to get back on the team.

They are going to think that it is heaven on earth. 'Are you kidding me? I don't have to deal with any of this stuff. That's great!' Give them about two - four weeks and they will come back crying.

They can change their attitude, but they have to want to. We cannot change it for them.

There is some fluidity with where people fall in the matrix, but most people will fall inside the coaching section. This block will be full of people. You will have one, or maybe two in the rock star section, and it is very seldom, but you may have one or two in the isolation section. If you get someone who falls in the 'fire them' section, if I were you, I wouldn't even wait for the week to end. Just make it easy, quick, and simple.

In Brian Gottlieb's book, Beyond The Hammer, his matrix is based on the sales professional's Performance vs Culture Fit. When the team member has performance issues, we manage through the KPIs. It's data driven metrics that keep us moving in the right direction and know where our bumpers are to assist in coaching that team member. However, when we have Culture Fit issues, those are coached through the mission and vision of the company and also determines if they should stay or be successful some place else.

When we look at building the right team, we have to look at the culture. Everyone has a different culture, but we call it the 'sales culture'. It is the culture inside that sales team.

In every team, we want to have team camaraderie. Together, we dominate, and divided, we fall.

We want to make sure that everyone is supported, and they support each other.

We don't want anyone to secretly hope another rep falls on their face.

If there was a lot of fighting, the last thing I would want them to do is to talk to each other on team text, so those are monitored.

We have team message boards and text boards where we talk all day long. We cheer them on when they make a sale, reps help other reps within those group messages, and we keep all the negativity off those boards.

If we have all the right players, we will have a team that is easy to train, easy to hold accountable, and easy to get buy-in from. They all are pushing for themselves, but also for the team and each other. That is the culture we are hoping for.

What is Your Sales Culture?

Inside the sales culture, we have to define what we want and interview for that sales culture.

They might look like a great salesperson, but if you don't feel that they would fit in with the culture, keep them out.

If what you are looking for is a very team-oriented, easy-to-hold accountable, fun, and easy-to-get along with person, and you are interviewing someone, and it sounds like they are a rock star, but not a team player, if you take that person and put them into the middle of your team, they will destroy your team.

He will come out awesome, and you are going to love him, but your team will get destroyed because you just put that person in the middle of a great culture. There will be other boiler room cultures where that person may fit beautifully.

When you have good team camaraderie in group communication, they will support each other if they need help. If they have a question, and the sales leader may not be available, then someone can jump in and say, "Yeah, I've had that before. I'm going to send you some supporting documents, or here is how you deal with that situation." They help each other out.

The other part of working together as a team is role play. This is when a sales rep goes back and forth with another sales rep to work on a certain skill with someone who excels at that certain skill. This doesn't always have to be with the sales leader. If one of the sales reps taught the closing roadmap, or how to do rebuttals, then one of the sales reps can ask, "Hey, Billy, do you think you can stay after with me for a little bit, or meet me for lunch? There was a skill that you did well, and I'd like to sit down with you and dive into that." It is that type of team camaraderie you want, where they don't mind going out afterward and work on getting better.

Some of these sales reps who I have worked with do not have the team camaraderie and say, "Man, I've got to work with these guys. I don't want to go out with them afterward too." Why? Do you hate them? I don't understand.

You have to know what your culture is before you draft your players.

If you hire a new sales leader, he first has to determine what type of culture there is right now. He is not going to be able to find that in the first month. This is something where he has to entrench himself in that organization because he might find out that the culture came from the organization itself.

If he wants a certain culture, but the organization is a completely different type of culture, it is going to be very tough. He might have to work with the owner and other managers to fix the company culture, or worst case, isolate his team from the rest of the organization.

This will take about 60-90 days to figure out what type of culture there is, and why, unless it is screaming obvious.

How Do You Find Your Sales Reps?

Before we fire someone, unless they need to go immediately, we will give them enough time and training to prove themselves. If it is very obvious that this person either doesn't fit the culture, or they are just not going to perform, you can let them go earlier. We do like to give everybody the benefit of the doubt and try to retrain them.

Even as a new sales leader, I like to try to retrain someone because you want to believe they can do the job, but many times I find out that I hit their ceiling. Once you hit a sales rep's ceiling, you either determine that you are okay with that ceiling, or it is time for them to go.

The right individuals are what make the sales culture. You hire and fire based on your culture. Here is a reason someone gets fired, maybe it is integrity, and maybe that is part of your culture. I would like to say everyone's culture has integrity, but unfortunately, that is not the case.

You hire and fire based on the culture that you want, or that you have.

We never stop looking for new sales reps. I like to be in a position where I only take rock stars because I don't need anyone. When you wait until you need reps, you will make your decisions based on the immediate need of just getting someone in that spot to handle leads.

How Do You Interview?

When picking our team, we have to set their expectations during the interview. We want them to know exactly what is expected of them when they come in.

We look at all kinds of things during the interview. We look at how they came to the door, and how they interacted with the gatekeeper.

What did they do in your lobby while they were there? Did they just go sit down and stare at the wall? Did they strike up a conversation with the front desk person? Were they respectful to people they just met when walking in or did they ask for you and just sat down as if the people up front weren't important?

Did they go straight over and look at your accolades, and maybe some pictures on the wall that show what you have done as a company, like the awards you have won? That is what we hope, that they want to learn as much as they can.

When we bring them back, how did they sit in the chair?

What kind of respect did they give you from the get-go? Did they disrespect you and slouch in the chair?

You want to know because that is exactly what they are going to do after today. That is how they are going to treat you, and that is how they are going to treat the customer.

Their character is what you are looking for and, a lot of the time, their body language is their character.

Are they just sitting there answering your questions, or are they engaging you and asking questions too? Are they inquisitive? Are they naturally curious people?

Did they sit down and act very confident?

Did they talk out of their throat? Did they mumble?

Did they look away? Did they not make eye contact?

What they do in the interview is so much more important than what they say. I put very little emphasis on their answers to my questions.

I am more interested in how they answered the questions.

We need someone who is going to come in, is very confident, and is going to do what needs to be done.

Setting Expectations For Sales Professionals

Expectations are set in three categories, and these three categories are performance-based, admin-based, and self-development.

The performance-based are their KPIs, and these are where your benchmarks and targets are. These are how you are expected to perform.

The admin-based is your paperwork. You are expected to turn in clean contracts. You are expected to take the right pictures. You are expected to do the videos. These are all the things that you are expected to do that you don't typically make money on. This is the administrative part of your job. Other examples of administrative expectations would be, Make sure all daily notes are in the CRM by midnight. Get all corrections completed within 24-72 hours.

There is also the aspect of self-development. We are going to continue to work with them, but they have to accept that type of training from us. We want to see them grow into better individuals and better leaders, even though they may never be a leader. We want to grow them into that type of leader so that they are willing to jump into the gap and help other sales reps or help the customer.

There are many times when we have to back up the customer because the production department wants to do it one way, and the customer wants to do it another way. Sometimes we have to come to the rescue of the customer as a sales rep because production can often push a homeowner around.

Many times we have to do the same thing with production. As Nathan Tebedo says in his speech, The Hero Sales Culture, We come and stand in the gap with the production department because the homeowner is coming at production in a certain way.

How Do You Assess Them?

I like to do an assessment of a potential employee before I ever even do an interview. Before we send them the interview date, we want them to take the assessment because when I interview them, that assessment may change the questions that I ask.

It doesn't matter what assessment you use, and they are all very good. There is the Dominance, Influence, Steadiness, and Conscientiousness, or DISC Assessment, the Objective Management Group, or OMG Assessment, and there are what are called 'one-question assessments'.

These assessments help you find out what you are not seeing during the interview process. What are they not telling you?

With a DISC Assessment, I know that if they have a high 'D', and a high 'I', they can be great at in-home sales, and they have an Ego. They are not going to fold when a customer says a price is too high. They are talkative, and at least they are intelligent enough to have a decent conversation. That is their 'I'.

I need them to have a low 'S', which means submissive. They need to have, at least, a below-average 'S'. I would rather them have an above average 'C', which is their ability to do paperwork. That is the analytical piece of them.

If they are very submissive, I am going to bring it up with them. My dominant is off the charts. Yet, I am very docile in front of a homeowner because obviously, I know how to sell. There are others that their dominance is off the charts, and they are just a total asshole in the house. That is not what we want. We want someone with emotional intelligence.

We also have an assessment for emotional intelligence. This is typically done after you are hired. We can train for EQ, but for character, we cannot.

We want to know who you are before you come in, as far as the character itself.

Be careful putting too much weight on these assessments. They are simply there to assist you in the decision, not to make the decision for you.

How to Build a Strong Bench of Players

Knowing how many sales reps you need is pertinent to your success.

You will have that number, and then you need to add a certain number to that based on your trade because people get sick, people will have low performance, and people go on vacation. You want to make sure that when you put someone on the bench, you have someone else to put into their position.

Let's say someone has poor performance or a poor attitude. We need to take them, put them on the bench, and work with them. Meanwhile, someone else has taken their spot while they are being retrained.

If you have just enough to run the appointments that you would typically have, then the tail is going to wag the dog.

The sales reps know that, and they will take advantage of it every time. They know that you can't let them go, so they are going to do whatever they want, and they know you can't do anything about it.

Take that away from them, and make sure that you have a strong bench and that you have sales reps ready to take the top rep's positions.

People get scared that they are going to hire someone, and then not be able to feed them leads. You will need to lower the leads for everyone else if they are good enough to be on the team. You can also go to the marketing director or owner and let them know the number of additional leads you need.

If you have a strong bench, and you don't need new reps, that is when the top-performing reps come out of the woodwork. For whatever reason, they come alive when you don't need them. They come walking through the front door.

If you are desperate for sales reps, like if someone quit, and you are thinking, 'Oh my gosh, I need someone right now', then you are going to pick a fresh body because that is all that is available to you, and that is all that you are going to see.

If you don't really need anyone, and you just keep looking, making sure that you don't pass anyone up, then you are going to start seeing some excellent talent come your way because you do not need them.

If we needed five sales reps to hit our goal, I would most likely go out and get eight.

You never know where that 'hot hand' is going to be, it could be a brand-new rep, or it could be someone you never expected.

A hot hand means that they are selling everything that they touch. We want to feed them as many appointments as we can. Their tenure doesn't matter. I don't care if they have been there 20 years or 20 days.

We feel that, if you have momentum, and that energy is coming out, you are motivated, and you are excited. When you sell a job, you are going to sell the next one because you just sold the last one.

We see that as a hot hand. That person is selling, and they are selling very well. This is like the law of inertia. Things at rest tend to stay at rest, and things in motion tend to stay in motion.

Now that they are in motion, and they are moving much faster, they are selling better. As long as they keep their head in the right place, they will continue that positive momentum. The moment someone disrupts that, they will start to stumble, and they will start losing momentum.

There is a thing that we call quicksand in our industry. Quicksand is when you do something wrong, and something bad happens, and then something else happens, and then something else happens. Before you know it, you are sinking into this quicksand, and you can't seem to get yourself out of it. We notice it as sales leaders, and we hope that they notice it as sales reps, and we try to stop it.

We are going to take you out of the field, and we are going to go back through some basic retraining, and we are going to send you out with somebody with a hot hand because we want you to get back into that groove of selling.

We want to get you back into the motivation and the excitement of someone else who is selling, and all of a sudden, now that you are getting back into it, you are selling again.

When I came to work with Able Roofing, they were closing at 28%, and they had some very strong sales talent, but they were all doing something different to sell. They were all selling and closing their own way.

I knew that I could come in and get rid of people who shouldn't be there, retrain the people who were there, set new expectations, and let them know how the culture was going to look there.

I let them know that if they felt like they didn't like that culture, or new expectations, the door is over there. I am going to high-five you on the way out, and I am going to wish you the best of luck. We didn't have anyone leave like that, but we did have to let a few people go that didn't fit the culture over time. For the most part, they came together as a team and were looking for that.

The President was nervous that I was going to come in and disrupt things like, 'Hey, you can't change things'. 'These guys are set in their ways'.

They weren't set in their ways, they were just looking for guidance. They were looking for that ability to be a team, but no one had previously cared much about the team.

When I came in, the team at that location was very welcoming, and it was easy to get along with them. It only took six months to go from a 28% close rate, which means they closed 28% of the appointments they ran, to over 60%. Now they have expectations, training, and accountability.

Sales reps love black and white, and they hate gray. Sales reps hate gray because gray just gives them enough rope to hang themselves.

If they know what they are supposed to do, how they are supposed to do it, that we can prove that they will win by doing it and that we will get their buy-in, we will have a much better team and a much better outcome.

I built that team to a level that they had never seen before. They have never seen that level of performance in any of their locations before.

When I have the right players, it gives me confidence, and I get to have fun too.

When I know that my team has been picked, I am satisfied. I like my team, and I would even use the word 'love' for my team. It makes my job easy. I don't have as much stress, and that is huge for us.

In sales, we have a ton of stress. If you want to eliminate some of that stress, pick the right players because then having the right team is one less thing you have to worry about.

At that point, I had to keep 25 plates spinning because there were 25 sales reps, and I had to monitor each one of them, go out with each one of them, and get to know each one of them. I had to get their buy-in of me so that they could come to me when they had an issue, and I didn't have to guess when they had an issue because their numbers were going to show it. This made my life easier.

If you have the right team, the right training, and the right processes, you will be a very bored sales leader, which is good. You keep doing what you are supposed to be doing, but you are not constantly having things pop up.

With most companies that we go into, either the sales leader doesn't even know that he has emergencies all around him, and he is just oblivious, or he has them and doesn't know how to deal with them, or has so many fires to put out that is all they do all day long. They are also just professional firefighters. 'Man, I've just got all of these fires to put out with no time for anything else'.

Did you know that you started all those fires that you are putting out?

You started them by not being preventative. You are a reactive leader. It is important to understand if you are a reactive leader or a proactive leader.

Are you a firefighter? Because if you are, your team is never going to go anywhere. You are going to be the team's hero all the time, but you don't want to be the team's hero all the time. If you are the team's hero, they depend on you for everything. You are there for support, and they know that you are always going to back them up. But if all you're doing is putting out fires, that means there is very little leadership, otherwise there wouldn't be fires, or they would learn to handle those fires themselves.

Fires start from poor leadership. Sales professionals either don't know any better and make poor decisions based on the lack of direction given by leadership, or they feel they can get away with something due to experience of being able to get away with it in the past.

Sales reps, when they are part of a great team with the right players, have a great support system. It is not just about the leaders and the organization. It is about the leaders on the team, and you have great leaders when you have a great team. You have people that are willing to step up and help.

There have been many times when, in the sales meeting, the question is asked, and I am going to answer, but someone else jumps in. I am going to let them have a conversation right there in the middle of the sales meeting, and I want a sales rep to answer another sales rep's question. Yeah, I can answer it, but when another sales rep steps in and answers that constructively, we know that we have a good team, or at least some of the guys on the team are good and willing to help when needed.

This is your team. So, make it your team.

When the football draft happens, they pick the best players. They pick the best players because they want to win.

You need to go out and pick the best players because you want to win. Draft your players.

Chapter 4

TAKING OVER THE CASTLE

What are you committed to achieving?

It's time to put together your SEAL Team 6. You need the best of the best when it comes to sales.

It's time to take over the castle with the people you have chosen, and the goals you have made.

You better have the right people. Did you pick them because they happen to be breathing, or did you pick them because they deserve to be on the team?

Also, when we say we are going to storm the castle, we need to have a clear plan of how we are going to do it.

What are we going to do? What is the new strategy? We have to be ready for this.

We have to have our whole sales process ready. Whether you are going to use my sales process or one of the 150 other sales processes out there, don't worry, they all work. Some are better than others, but you just need to make sure which you will master. Our process is more modern and easy to look like an expert in your field.

I shouted that out, even on stage, and people laughed, and they asked, "Aren't you supposed to sell your sales process?"

Sales are effortless, just look around.

If you have ever heard, "If it was easy enough, everybody would do it." That's B.S. Because everyone is doing it, and it is not hard.

There are only a few ways of doing it, and when you look at all these different sales processes, they are all very similar.

You are going to go through the entire process. You are going to make sure that they are comfortable with your product or service in one way or another.

Then, because you know that your prices are higher than anyone in the market, you are going to condition them on price so that their expectation of the price will be much higher. Then, we will deliver the proposal and understand how to close it.

We have sales leaders write out their mission, and at the top of this, it says, 'If there's no mission, there's no position.' Then underneath it says, 'What is your mission?'

When we talk about storming the castle, what is your mission, and how will you succeed in this position?

Inside the mission is where they write out what they feel is expected of them and what their plan is.

That mission changes, that mission can change every 30 days, it can change quarterly, it definitely changes yearly.

What is that mission? How are they going to storm that castle? They have to write that out.

The mission can be so many different things. It can be that you are taking on a storm that just happened, or figuring out what your mission is.

'How are we going to take this storm on?' or 'How are we going to take on this new level of success?'

You have to first figure out what that mission is and what is at the end of it. Start with the end in mind. Then we work our way back to find out the strategies and battle plans we need to put in place.

When someone talks about how they are supposed to hit a certain number, we have to break that number down, and we have a spreadsheet that does this.

The overall mission is that, in a certain year, we need that sales leader to hit, for example, $10 million. If they do not exactly know how they are going to hit this goal, the first thing that we do is we have them write in the first four years, January through December, and then we find their trend in the form of what we call 'bell curves'.

Not every month is the same, but there is a very evident trend year over year. We just need to find out what that is. Now that we know what the bell curve is, I put in my goal, and all the numbers for each month come in.

Determining the mission has to be the first step for a sales leader to take over the castle, and then determining who they are going to take in and who is going to be on the team.

Determining the strategy that will be used is also important. I even call this 'Breaking The Barrier'. It's like a road map to going past what you thought was possible.

This road map is your bell curve, the road map is breaking down the numbers.

Once we have those numbers, we have to make sure that the sales reps are all moving in the same direction, that they have all been trained in the same system, and that they know the sales system.

We train our team, and then we determine what that roadmap is, which is where we break the numbers down not only for the team, but we break them down for each individual and each department in the company. This is a team effort, not just a sales team effort. The phone room, the marketing department, and the sales department are all working together. This is all part of the roadmap.

In many companies, they do not talk, or even like each other. The phone room, the marketing department, the sales department, and the production department, for that matter, just do not get along. They tend to blame each other for everything that goes wrong.

As leaders, we need to mend those fences, we need to put the grenades away and come together as a team and agree on where we are going to go and how we will get there.

Each piece of the mission is done daily. This is a game of inches, as many people would say. You cannot let one day go and just get to the next, you have to win each day, and you have to win each week.

The biggest mistake that most sales teams make is that they have a monthly goal, and they do not even look at the goal until the last week of the month, and they do the same thing quarterly and yearly.

This is why we have to win the day.

Whether we want to say ‘carpe diem’ or not, we have to seize the day.

If we look at each inch, or we look at every day, we win each day. The month is either easily won, or we are going to exceed our monthly goal by quite a bit.

Once we reach our goals, we do not exhale. We celebrate the wins, but we do not celebrate them exhaling or with a sigh of relief. If you do, before you know it, the next month is crap.

They exhale because they feel like they have exhausted themselves in the last month, but that was last month, and we have another month to plow through.

It is like a football game. If after the first half, the team that is winning says, “Man, we just won that half. Let’s celebrate!” and they exhale, they don’t think about the fact that there is a whole second half.

It is important to create a mission when the sales leader is new. You need to make your own mission. If you make your own mission, you are more likely to achieve it. If you make your own mission, that launch pad becomes more real.

You have to think of it as something big. This is a castle and a huge thing that you need to conquer. People often ask, "How do you eat an elephant?" The answer is, "One bite at a time."

Where are you going to start? At what point are you going to start? It is all based on the fact that you have this enormous task in front of you. We need to break this task down, and we need to get started now.

Just like when we schedule appointments, every day or every time frame that goes by without being scheduled, that is money that just goes into the ether. We lose that opportunity.

So, are we losing an opportunity while you are still trying to figure out what your purpose is? Are you losing opportunities by wandering around, still trying to figure out what your job is?

Let's put it on paper. Let's put the mission to work.

It is about my mission, my position, my purpose, and what's expected of me.

Usually, when I am brought in, it is to take on the impossible.

If most sales leaders were to see a lot of what I am given when I go into an organization, they would see it as impossible.

What I do from there is break all the numbers down to understand what is needed and who I need on the team to make that possible.

When I went into American WeatherTechs, we started with a decent team. We hired more members and made a strong bench.

Even so, we still could not affect the close rate like we wanted to. We brought up the close rate, and we definitely brought up sales, but the close rate was not where we needed it to be. I knew that even though we were making record numbers of sales revenue, my close rate was still low, and I could not say that I was winning.

Even though I was winning monthly with the revenue numbers, I was not winning because I was not taking advantage of the opportunities in front of me. Please hear me when I say, revenue is a liar. Revenue is a false number until you get into all of the other numbers behind it. The most important number being the profit. I have seen many organizations have huge months where they didn't make any money at all. They even celebrate it because they don't have processes in place to show the other numbers that tell you if you really did well or not.

When we started to look at who was on our team, the missing piece was the phone room. We still had admin and owners scheduling calls. They were all very busy, and they did not have time to sit there on the phone and get the needed information from the prospect to effectively allow a sales rep to go out and close the deal.

Once we realized this, we put a phone room into play, and it completed the team. Our close rate shot up, our revenue shot up even more, and our ability to hit a much higher number was complete.

That felt amazing. That is when, behind closed doors, we can celebrate.

If you are a sales leader who is just starting on a mission, what you have to look forward to is not only a job well done but a new understanding of how to win. It is the experience of understanding what it takes to be great.

You cannot be great until you have been great, and I really feel that way.

Until you know what it takes to be great and to be at the top of that mountain, knowing that there are bigger mountains to climb, this is a mountain that you conquered.

It is not exactly Everest, but it is going to feel like it.

Determining the Mission

Determining the mission is going to be different for every sales rep.

This is why we make them come up with their own mission. They have the numbers in front of them, and they have the expectations of the owner in front of them, but they are the ones who have to figure out what their mission is. They have to ask themselves, 'What does my castle look like? What does this mountain that I want to climb look like?' They also need to understand what it looks like to win.

When we hit this goal, what would it look like? There has to be emotion to this because if there is no emotion to winning, it is like getting a hole in one when no one is around. You do not have anyone to share it with.

Once you get this, no one wants to celebrate until the end of the year when we know that we have hit our mission, then you can look at your team and smile. We did it. We not only hit this goal, we blew it away. Every month that you hit it, you get to nod at each other and say, "Alright, we got this one. Now for next month."

You have your expectations of the owner, but the mission has to come out of you. Just like a sales leader selling an idea to the team or team member.

You have to make this mission your idea. Something that you feel is big enough that you are willing to lose sleep over, that it is big enough that you are willing to get up early in the morning. Even more important than that is that you realize you truly have to win the day.

This gives you a drive, and you would truly get upset if you did not do what you were supposed to. There are people who just do not care and say things like, "We'll do it next month."

Next month? We are only halfway through this month, and you are already thinking about next month because you don't think you are going to win this month.

You have to want it so bad that you know every day is a win, and that every inch is a win.

This is what most people get wrong. Most sales leaders sit back and act like success is just going to come, it's just around the corner. If they do not win, it's because the number is too high. It is not a gimme.

If you don't win throughout the day, if you don't know where your people are, or if you don't know where you're going to end each day and each week, you are going to lose.

If there is no consequence for losing, then you will not care. I am not saying beat yourself up about it, but you should still be passionate about winning, so passionate that it eats at you. If you are so passionate about winning, you are actually going to care about who is on your team.

The sales leader has to be passionate about winning. When things go wrong people say, 'The speed of the leader is the speed of the gang.'

If the sales leader thinks, 'Oh, I'm going to lead by example, I am going to go out and sell' to show them how good I am. They will listen to me.

'The speed of the leader is the speed of the gang' means that if you care, maybe they will care. That is why we need the right people, the right attitude, and people running in the same direction.

Leading by example for a leader is showing you have the discipline and accountability that you are asking from your team. Not that you should steal opportunities from your team and sell them.

Who Are You Bringing Onto Your Team?

Now that you have the team, and they are motivated, you need to turn up the heat.

They already have the right attitude, and we are just pushing them in the right direction. There has to be a certain amount of pressure put on everyone.

You may think that your team is the sales team that I am talking about, but it is not, I am talking about the entire team.

If you are a sales leader, and you are in charge of sales, your sales team is just a part of the success of the sale. It is also the phone room, the marketing department, and the production department.

When we look at the team, we need to put a certain amount of pressure on each part of the team. We have to put the expectations into that team. They have to know what their mission or their job within this mission is.

If one part of that team does not do their job, then someone else has to work twice as hard. There is a phrase that I cannot stand, which is, 'Your emergency is not my priority', and I am going to tell you that yes, it is.

If they did not do their job, you still have yours. You cannot go to the owner and say, "Well, they didn't do what they were supposed to do, so I couldn't do what I am supposed to do."

As a sales leader, you cannot say that. If I was an owner and a sales leader came to me and said, "Well, they didn't get me the right leads," I would say, "What did you do about it? Did you go to the marketing department and explain what it is that you need?" If not, don't you think you should have?

It is about taking ownership of the sales goal. It doesn't matter what the circumstances are, you still have numbers to hit.

As I wrote above, you are dependent on not just your sales team but the supporting teams as well.

We bring those people into the mission by breaking the numbers down and helping them understand that they have to be involved in the strategy.

When I ask sales leaders about the most important number that they see in our business, it is funny because they always say it is the 'sales needed', but that is the least important. The most important number is the 'leads needed'. So does your marketing department know that number? Or do they just know what the traffic is and giving themselves high-fives while you are still trying to decide how you're going to hit your sales goal.

If I don't have what I need coming in through the front door, nothing else is going to matter. If I don't tell them that in July, I need 211 leads, they are never going to get it. This is why I say that we need to bring everyone into this mission. If there is one person who does not know their part of the mission, then it destroys everything.

The team and their influence are always bigger than what most new sales leaders realize. Sales leaders just think that they are going to tend to their flock like they are shepherds. They are walking around with a stick, just making sure that everyone stays in line.

Keeping your team moving is a small part of what you do. A good sales leader is the communication, or the grease, between all other departments.

The sales leader marries the other departments in many cases.

If we are going to talk about the team, we have to talk about everyone on the team. If you look at the team as just the sales team, what you are getting ready for is that you are going to start throwing grenades over the wall, saying, "Well, you didn't get me enough leads," or "You guys didn't ask the right questions when you got them on the phone."

You are throwing these grenades over the wall and throwing blame because you did not hit your goal, saying, 'It has got to be the phone room because they book bad appointments', or 'Maybe it is the marketing not getting us enough leads. If they had given me the leads, we would have gotten the sales we needed.'

At the end of the day, you are the one who is holding the 'goal' and holding the football.

I have heard many times when people talk about how the coaches are the ones that have their names in the magazine or the newspaper. They say, 'If the guy in the booth made the right call, then we would not be talking about Belichick here.'

No, Belichick was the one holding the whole team, and he was the leader. Many people look at this and think that it is the owner. No, the owner is in the box, just watching the game. You are the sales leader, you are the one on the field, and you are the one that is blamed if anything is to go wrong.

Why not get your team in order?

Winning isn't hard, just remember that you have people that are willing to work with you as long as you work as a team. No blame can be pushed around when the team works together towards the same goal. Remind everyone that we all have our part of the plan and if we all help each other hit our goals, hitting the company goals and even the BHAG (Big Hairy Audacious Goal) becomes easy.

Forecasting: Determining the Road Map

In our industry, we have to find our bell curve.

You cannot say, 'I have twelve months, so I am going to take my overall goal and divide it by twelve.' You cannot do that. You are never going to sell as much in January as you would in March, for example.

Every company may be a little bit different. I will say that in most cases, it is region-specific, but every company is different based on the way that they market, and the way that they sell.

Knowing that we now know our bell curve, we now know what every month should be. I first have to break it down by the month to know what I am looking at. This is what we would call our 'conservative goal'.

This is what the sales leader must hit ultimately to keep their job. You have to have a conservative goal for your budget. You have to hit this to hit your budget.

When we are talking to a sales rep, we ask, 'What would change your life?', but when we are looking at a company, we say, 'I know you want to do five million, but what do you really want to do? What would really make you celebrate?' That is our BHAG, explained below.

We then break it down even further. Just having those numbers is great, but now, how do you do it?

We have to look at their KPIs, their key performance indicators, their lead-to-appointment, and where the raw lead and conversion ratio comes into the appointment.

We need to look at what is known as a 'big, hairy, audacious goal', or BHAG, an idea from Jim Collins in his book 'Built to Last'.

There is a saying that if I shoot for the moon, I will hit some stars. If all you are doing is shooting for that conservative goal, I promise you will not hit it.

If you shoot for that BHAG instead, you will at least hit your conservative goal, if not more.

Owners often focus heavily on their marketing percentage, saying things like, "I have to keep it at 10%." But if the company fails to hit its budgeted revenue goal, that percentage can easily jump to 18% or even 20%, which severely cuts into profitability.

What we have found is that when we push that BHAG or that higher goal, they hit that conservative goal every time.

They can either come up with it to say, 'That is really what I'd like to hit', or they can take a look at that and say, 'I'm going to go ahead, and I'm going to go 20% more.'

What we typically recommend is to hit, on average, 20% higher than your conservative goal depending on where you currently are. Throughout the year, we only look at that larger number. We look at our conservative goal to make sure that we are within that area, but we are focused on that larger number.

I've found that a lot of the home improvement industries look at a good number for marketing percentage as 10%. When you look at how much you are going to spend in marketing, and if you are going to do a million dollars, then you are going to spend $100,000 in marketing. If I go based on my BHAG goal, then I am going to get myself in trouble with a higher marketing percentage. So we are going to put that at 10% of their budget goal, but we will shoot for the BHAG.

You should have an overall strategy because if you don't, there is no way you are taking over that castle, and there is no way you are going to hit anything that even resembles the numbers that you expected at the end of the year. You won't even come close to it.

A lot of sales departments have that goal, and then they just do their best. They have absolutely no idea what number they should hit that month.

Earlier today, I got off the phone with a brand-new client, who said, "Yeah, we are doing well. We are going to hit half a million dollars."

I thought, 'with what they need to hit for the year, that is grossly underperforming'.

He thinks that he is killing it, and that is the problem.

If you do not know what you should be hitting, you may think that anything is better than what you did last year.

Another part of that strategy and roadmap is, once you know how many people are needed on the team, you need to determine how you are going to train them.

What am I going to do with these people, now that I have them?

How am I going to hold them accountable for hitting the goals that we put in place?

Each member of your team should have Conservative and BHAG monthly goals to hit also. We ask them what would change your life? That would be their BHAG. Once you come up with all of their monthly numbers, now break them into weekly numbers. Those are the numbers they need to see. Sales reps need to be focused on daily and weekly goals, not monthly goals.

If they are focused on monthly numbers, they don't look at the score until the last week of the month and it's too late, they have already lost control of the month.

We have made the TOP REP Forecasting spreadsheet available to you. Simply go to: go.topreptraining.com/book-resources

Celebrate, But Don't Exhale

We have to keep pressure on the team so that we can hit those numbers.

Once we hit our end goal, we celebrate in such a way that we are happy with what we did, but we can't have a party or act in front of the team as if we just hit some big accomplishment. Save that for the end of the year.

We have the right people, the right number of people, and we know our numbers. A lot of this has to do with everything else that we do.

That means holding them accountable, having the sales meetings, and having morning calls called 'power hours', so that we keep them on track.

You have to keep your team engaged, and you have to keep the pressure on the team.

The moment you take pressure off the team, they start to scatter and start to do their own thing. They will not know what to do next.

Let's say that we are a football team, we get to halftime, and we celebrate our performance for that half.

Then you go back out, and the other team just walks all over you the last half of the game because you exhaled.

Instead, you should go in, happy with the fact that you are ahead, but say, 'Guys, we have got another half. We have to keep going, we have to do it better. We know that they are strategizing right now, and we have to go out there and do better than we did the first half.'

We did not allow anyone to exhale. They still have that pressure on, and they are still ready to go.

There is a great story about Florida/Ohio State football coach, Urban Meyer, who won several national titles. After one such victory, everybody was celebrating in the locker room. He walked straight through the locker room, got right into his office, and started calling next year's recruits right away.

He says, 'We won the game, it is time to get ready for next year.'

While everybody was screaming and yelling, he was getting ready for next season.

There is never the time to exhale.

Exhaling means that you are satisfied and ready to take a bit of a break. You worked hard enough, you are tired, and you are going to go sit on the couch.

Unfortunately, that 'couch' in our industry takes the form of a month. Sales reps do this all the time, where they crush it for a month, and then come back down the next month.

We call them 'roller coaster reps' because they are up and down. There are also 'roller coaster leaders' who are the ones who hit the month hard, and they are exhausted by pushing their team. They take the pressure off the team for the next month, thinking that they do not have to worry anymore. The whole team comes down as well, because their leadership decided that they were going to take a bit of a break.

You can prevent that by not exhaling. Know that once you are done with this month, you are already on to the next month. It's ok to let everyone know they have done a great job but that month is already behind us.

When we are in August, I am in September and October as a sales leader. I know that I am holding my sales reps accountable for every day in August, but I am planning for September and October already so that by the time that hits, everything is ready for the team to be successful.

Again, we give everybody high-fives that they did a job well done, but it is not time to exhale, it is already the next month. This is a very, 'What have you done for me lately?' type of business. Yesterday never matters, what happened last month does not matter. That was last month, and that might as well have been last year.

If a sales leader has made every point, and they are celebrating and not exhaling, they took down that castle, and they are already on to the next castle. It is like a video game of a series of twelve castles that they need to take down.

Every time you go into a month, it is going to be an unfamiliar month. You may have never hit a number this big before in August. You may have hit it in July, but this is August, it is a different month. Last August, your goal was maybe $100,000 less than this month. It is a whole new castle, a whole new thing that you have to be ready for.

I have taken down the next castle every month for the last 20 years, and it is exciting, but it can be stressful at the same time. It seems like there is never time to celebrate. You did it, and it is great that you did, but even when you finish the year, come January 1st, that was last year.

It can be stressful, and it can be exhausting, but that is what we sign up for. The top sales leaders in the industry know that today is just another day to win.

If you were to look at your team and if you were to put a number on everyone there, of what they made before they ever joined this team, many of these people have never made more than $30,000 - $50,000 in their life.

Some of them have their GED, some have just gotten out of the military, and some of them have college degrees and upwards of a Ph.D. or a Master's. It is funny how many different people you have.

When you look at these folks who have a GED, who never made that much money, or are coming out of the armed forces having no idea what they want to do, now making more than what most doctors and lawyers make, realize, 'you just changed someone's life'. At the end of the day, at the end of the year, I look at them.

When I get to celebrate, it is me watching my team. As a coach, I get to watch 100 teams, the stories that come in, and the things they get to do.

One of the top sales representatives in the country and his wife sold $18.5 million, which is approximately $1.8 million in commissions. He was working at Pizza Hut about 24 years ago. He worked his way up to this, but I will also tell you, I do not think he has ever had a sales year that he has not made at least a quarter of a million dollars or more.

He worked his way up. We found him when my partner, Jim Johnson, played one-on-one ball with him and asked him if he wanted a job. Jim saw some determination in him and offered him a position in roofing sales, and he only took that position to help him get through school. Then, when he found out how much money he could make, he put the effort into it.

Now he is currently one of the highest-producing in-home sales professionals in the country.

When we say taking over the castle, we are not just looking at the typical goal. We want this massive commitment that is sitting in front of us, and that is why we look at it as a castle. If we are going to take this thing over, it has to be something big.

When we look at this big commitment, we look at breaking down and determining what that mission is, we are going to find out who we are taking with us, and then we have to figure out what the strategy is.

How are we going to do this?

We have to look at it completely broken down. Too many people look at it, and say, 'We are going to do the best we can.' The thing that most people don't understand is that doing your best is like when you tell your kids, "Hey, just do your best." You really want your kids to do their best, and they take that into their adult years, but what they don't understand is that your best is very seldom good enough.

You have to do better than what you feel your best is.

People look at self-limiting beliefs and say, "I did my best." How do you even know what your best is? Did you truly go to absolute exhaustion, or did you just go to where it was uncomfortable?

We, as sales leaders, are given these commitments. I hate common goals, which are commitments that we have to meet. Some of them are big, so we have to break them down.

I cannot go to the owner and say, "Well, I did my best." I am sure that he is not going to pat me on the head like when I was a kid and say, "I know you did your best."

Seeing it as a castle gives the sales leader an understanding that you do not underestimate the task at hand, and you do not underestimate what you are looking at.

If I am supposed to hit ten million in sales this year, most sales leaders, just like sales reps, do not look at it until November. We have to break it down, and we have to have that strategy.

Why go through this? Why is it worth it? For one, it can change your life but also the lives of the people on your team and their families.

I did an exercise with some of the Amish guys that I work with. I said, "I know that right now you do not really know what you are doing and why you are doing it, but let's look at it this way, how many people are in the company?"

I think he said that there are 26 people in the company.

I wrote the number 26, and I said, "You affect 26 lives. If you don't sell it, then they cannot produce it. These people have a job that they could not have elsewhere. You are not only affecting 26 people but, on average, how big are their families?"

Granted, those Amish have big families, but we found out that we are affecting up to 100 to 150 people. I then said, "Now you're affecting the lives of 150 people because you decided to take a job."

Again, when you are looking at being the sales leader, you have your sales teams, but you also have everybody else in the company and their families. You get to look around because when they are hitting numbers that the company has never hit before, these families are living like they have never lived before.

That is why we do it. That is why when I look at the next month, it is not just a number to me. If I can do this, if I can lead this team to be able to hit this goal, then this team and their families will be able to live as they have never lived before, better than they have lived before.

We all get to go to the next level, not just the owner.

Chapter 5

GREASING THE WHEELS

Being a leader and giving effective servant leadership is about greasing the wheels and giving people what they need to effectively work together and succeed.

When I am working, if I don't give someone what they need, they can't do their job. Even though they are there to support me, if I say, "I just need you to set this up," and he doesn't know how I want it set up, he wouldn't be able to do his job effectively.

From that to the sales reps, I have to make sure that they have everything they need to go and, as I said previously, take over the castle.

We have to also give them the tools, whether it is the electronics that they need, or the tool belts and tool bags. That is what I call 'greasing the wheels', or what you might call servant leadership.

If you are going to be effective at 'greasing the wheels', the team as a whole has to trust you, and that is where servant leadership comes in. They want to know that you are in it for them, that you have their best interest in mind, and you are going to give them what they need.

The easiest way to earn their trust is, for one, integrity. Do what you say you are going to do, and then, two, get them what they need. Make sure that they have what they need to be successful. The only way you can grease the wheels is to show the team that you do care about them, and that you're willing to stick up for them.

In my experience, there were many times when a sales rep did what they were supposed to do but somewhere along the line, a ball was dropped with a client. In the back office, they wanted to take everything from the sales rep, saying, "They never seem to get it right, they have to pay for all of their mistakes."

I said, "First, I need to do my due diligence. I want to find out what is going on before you take anything from the sales rep. If I see that it truly is the sales rep's fault, then I will go to the sales rep, and I will let them know."

However, many times it is not the sales rep's fault. It is someone else who may have dropped the ball, whether it is the production department or something down the line of giving it to the production department. We had to back up the sales rep and let them know that the sales rep did their job and that they deserved full compensation.

This is one of those instances where we stick up for the sales reps. When the company wants to once again change the compensation, it is always on the sales reps. It is so easy to change the sales reps' compensation because it is usually on a percentage basis. They don't want to mess with production, they don't want to mess with admin, so it is always the sales reps that will take the hit. As sales leaders, we have to do what we can to back up the sales reps. They have to know that we have their best interest in mind.

Greasing the wheels is a show of faith to the sales reps, and it is a show of support, like the old saying, "People don't care how much you know until they know how much you care."

Ultimately, they couldn't care less about how smart I am in sales or know about what I am doing until they know that I care about each one of them.

We also have to look at communication itself.

Your people cannot be afraid to communicate with you. Often, in our industry, the sales reps are scared to talk to their sales leader.

They are scared of saying the wrong thing, they are nervous about asking a question that maybe they have asked before, and worried that the sales leader is just going to blow up on them or take opportunities away from them.

The other part of leadership is understanding empathy and sympathy. The sales leader sometimes shows too much sympathy, which means that they are going to coddle their sales reps. This is almost like I am talking out of both sides of my mouth. You cannot let them be scared to talk to you, but if you coddle them so much because of this, then they are going to just take advantage of you. They will never learn if all they have to do is come to you for everything and not do any research on their own.

Think of sympathy as taking their problems and making them yours. You have enough going on, you don't need your reps' problems also. However, if you show them empathy, you show them how to deal with their own issues and hand them back to the reps to deal with on their own. They will learn for next time and be better off in the long run.

Communication is one of the biggest issues within companies across America.

When communication becomes an issue, it's going to be poor communication or lack of communication that will cause your organization the most pain.

I understand if you have a large team, it can be very tough to be in constant communication with your team. This is one of the main reasons we suggest having no more than 8 reps under each sales leader. Having just 8 reps under you will enable you to keep in touch with everyone more regularly.

The line of communication always has to be there with everyone within the organization. I just had a client where the owner reached out to me and asked, "Do you know what is going on with the sales leader?"

I told them, "Well, I'm guessing everything's fine. I just talked to him yesterday."

The owner said, "Man, I don't know what's going on, but he just won't talk to me. I constantly communicate to all my leaders, but he just hasn't reached out to me."

When I talked to the sales leader, he said, "I'm just busy."

He let that owner's mind wander, and now all of a sudden, he thinks the worst, thinking, 'Does he want to be the sales leader anymore? Is he looking to quit? I wonder if he's looking elsewhere.'

This was all because he didn't reach out to him daily just to talk.

He just wants communication, and a lot of the sales reps want that as well.

I do a lot of communicating with our sales reps through our sales meetings. Inside our sales meetings, if what we are trying to accomplish is something that they need to know, we give it to them in writing through email or a handout. If we are going to go through house cleaning, we are not going to sit there and just tell them that certain colors have been discontinued, we are going to put it in writing so there is no misunderstanding and it doesn't take up valuable training time.

If you are going to change any processes, if you are going to give them information, and if you are going to inform them of certain things that are going on, give it to them in writing.

I am a huge introvert.

People think that is funny because I speak for a living. But if you see me off the stage, unless someone comes up to me, I don't go down and talk to people right away, it almost gives me anxiety. Yup, that's right, I speak in front of thousands of people monthly and crowds give me anxiety. Cue the laughter.

For me, even with my sales reps, If I am going to pick up the phone and make a phone call, it is going to be a very short phone call.

I am very intentional with anything that I say, and I don't typically have very long conversations unless there is a reason for the conversation.

I know sales leaders who only talk to their sales reps on Tuesdays at the sales meeting, which should not be the case. They need to know that you are always working. We all know that the majority of sales reps in our industry feel that their sales leader does absolutely nothing.

I will tell you, half of them are probably right, but the other half are working extremely hard, they are there at five o'clock in the morning, and they don't leave until about nine to ten o'clock at night. They are busy making sure that their team has everything that they need, that they are there when they need them, and that they are greasing the wheels.

If they are not talking to their sales reps, then they are in production, making sure that production has everything they need. They are making sure that marketing has everything they need, and that the phone room has everything they need.

When we look at sympathy and empathy, most sales leaders don't know the difference.

Sympathy is where you care so much about their problems and their issues that you are willing to put that monkey on your back. If they bring you a problem, you just let that monkey climb right onto your back, and you are going to go handle it ourselves.

If you do that, you are going to continue to handle that. They will say to each other, "Oh, if you have that issue, last time I just went and had Chuck deal with it."

I need them to deal with it because I have enough on my plate. That is sympathy, where you are sitting there listening to them and taking it on.

Empathy is listening, and then giving the problem back to them. You can advise them, you can help them in any way that you can, but you are going to hand that problem right back to them to solve.

You are not there to solve that problem for them.

There was a skit when we were kids, and we used to call it 'The Witch Doctor'.

When the skit starts, the witch doctor is standing there, and the first person comes in and says, "Doctor, my arm hurts."

The witch doctor looks at it, he touches the arm, and then the person says, "Oh my gosh, my arm feels amazing."

Then he walks out the back and then the witch doctor says, "Now my arm hurts."

Then the next person comes in and says, "Doctor, my stomach hurts."

The witch doctor touches the stomach, and the patient says, "Oh my gosh, I feel great," and he leaves.

Then the doctor says, "My stomach now hurts."

The next one comes in and says, "Doctor, I'm pregnant." Then the witch doctor runs out the back. (And everyone laughs.)

What am I trying to say with this anecdote? I'm illustrating sympathy. You are willing to take on everybody else's pain when you have sympathy, but with empathy, you are handing it back to them.

It is okay to use empathy as a leader. Instead of taking on their sickness, instead help them understand the problem and then send them back on their way to take care of that problem.

When I first started my management career, one of the owners said, "If you have the opportunity to be misunderstood, you will be." If you are not very clear with the instructions you give and how you give those instructions, they will misinterpret what you have to say and will still just do whatever it is that they want.

Again, this is all part of communication inside sales management. These are the things that they all need to understand.

Greasing the wheels means keeping the line of communication open. This brings back to what I mentioned previously about the fact that the sales leader needs to keep their phone on and that they cannot walk away.

As a sales leader, you cannot just tell your people, "Hey, just so you guys know, I'm not available after six."

If your people are working after six, you should be available after six. Keep those lines of communication open.

Give them lifelines.

A lifeline means that while they are on a sales call, and they need to reach out, they will have someone to go to for help.

This could be the sales leader, or if you have certain people on the team who are senior reps that agree that if they are not on a call, they don't mind taking a phone call from somebody, or a group text where they can say, "I need help."

If anyone sees that group text light up, everyone needs to jump in and see what they can do to help whoever is in the house.

This may be nothing more than, 'I need someone to give me a call, I need help with financing,' or whatever the case may be. It could be, 'Hey, does anybody know what this shingle is, or what's the cost of the new Moen handheld?' Whatever the case may be, they should be able to post in there and somebody will call or respond.

No matter what, they have to have the ability to have a lifeline or a support system.

There are so many times when I will put my heart into training these sales reps, but if we got to the next meeting, which is just one week away, and I tested them on it, every one of them would fail.

I trained them, they loved it, they thought it was great, but they just watched me. It was like I entertained them for two hours.

For example, if I show them how advanced skills in negotiating or emotional intelligence work, and get deep into it, after the meeting they talk about how great it was.

Then, when I go to them next week and say, "Alright, we're going to have a bit of a refresher," the guys all look at each other like they don't remember one thing about that.

However, if I am going to teach or train something, then I need to make sure that it sticks. The only way it is going to stick is if you teach and train it, you verify it, meaning that you are going to put it in writing, you are going to give it to them, and then let them know, "Next week we will be talking about this, and I do want to make sure that you guys know it. So use the week to study it. It's not good to be just average. We need to be ROCKSTARS."

We are not here to be average, and they need to know that.

When we look at how we are going to give information, whether it is in a sales meeting, a memo, or whatever the case may be, that is how it needs to happen.

Many times, we have this big talk in the sales meeting and no one writes anything down, and we know that no one picked up on anything.

It is good to motivate the team, but, if you don't put it in writing, and if you don't have them learn it, it is all for nothing.

Motivation is not something you can give someone.

You can turn the heat up, but they have to already be motivated. There has to already be a flame there to throw gas on the fire.

The key to motivation is understanding that at some point, they are already somewhat motivated, and the engine has already started.

They may not be moving, but that engine has started, they are excited, they are pumped, and we are just going to either hit the gas pedal or turn up the heat.

The sales management has to know the temperature of who your sales reps are and how you can turn on that motivation. This is done through questions, like requesting from the team, "Tell me something good." Asking them to share something positive that is happening in their life.

When I am going around the team and requesting, "Tell me something good. Tell me something that happened over the weekend that has you excited," I am trying to get that feeling going.

The other thing that we can do is show them a video, and it doesn't have to be a long video, but just something that turns the ignition on. There are so many motivational videos on YouTube that you can find that have something to do with your theme that week. Warning, don't show a video in every sales meeting. It gets to be expected and loses its effectiveness.

How to Fire Them Up

Your team has to be at least somewhat motivated for you to pump them up. If they are unmotivated, there is nothing that you are going to be able to do unless you win the lottery in front of them.

You can't fire up your team unless there is a flame already there.

But how do you fire them up?

We hire people because of their attitude, and we want to hire self-motivated people.

As long as they can trust you, then you can motivate them. If they cannot trust you, then you are not going to motivate anyone.

I would say 90-95% of core values start with integrity.

This is the most used word in all core values. If we start with integrity, we will have the ability to motivate our people.

Even if someone does not like you, as long as they know that you have integrity, they will get motivated.

Motivating your team is important because it brings positivity and excitement, and those things are what bring in sales.

We want our sales teams to be positive going into the houses.

I don't know if it is the law of attraction, but every one of us gives off energy. We are all made of electricity, and this is all explained by quantum physics.

For example, when I am at an airport, and I sit next to people, I will sometimes sit next to someone and I don't know why, but I just don't like them or I can feel their negativity. It almost gets to the point where my attitude starts to take a hit, and I start getting negative, so I will get up and move.

I don't even know what is going on in this person's life, but whatever it is, it is not good. Maybe they just got into an argument, and they are just angry, but they are putting off negative energy.

If a rep comes out of a sales meeting, and they are just mad at the world, because maybe you berated them in front of the team, or for whatever reason they are just very negative today, and you sent them to a client's house with that negative energy, their customers will feel it.

At that point, there is no way that they are going to sell anything. This is why we motivate them, this is why we bring that positivity, and this is why inside those sales meetings, we don't talk about anything negative.

One of the last things we do is pump them up right before they leave the room. You don't have to be a speech specialist to motivate your team.

I have seen a lot of sales leaders who have a really hard time motivating their teams. Many Sales Leaders are so boring that they couldn't motivate anyone if they were giving away a truck in the meeting. If they were to just say the right things, and do the right activities inside the sales meetings it could get the job done.

We have to motivate them so much that it lasts for the next seven days because on that eighth day, we are doing it again.

Tools for Success

When we give our team the tools, we are giving them the ability to succeed. We are giving them everything they need to go in and come out with a new client.

There are several types of tools. The job is very much based on the customer's perception of me, my product, and the company. But most of all, their perception of our solution to their problem.

This perception has to be won by what I look like, what I sound like, what I say, and what I do.

We have tools for that, but we also have physical tools that we give them to use that will build urgency, trust, and it will make them look like an expert.

We mandate that all of our sales reps have either a tool pouch or a tool belt, depending on the trade. The reason behind this is that we give the perception that 'we are the experts'.

This is very easy because the tools are a symbol of being an expert. But there are often sales reps who are too lazy, and leave that tool pouch or tool belt in their truck, and when they lose the sale they get upset.

If you go in looking like everyone else, and sounding like everyone else, then you are no different from anyone else.

We have to give them the tools for success. This is in the knowledge that you give them, as well as, in this case, the physical tools that you give them, that give them the ability to succeed.

It is like giving a baseball player a bat. He can't play baseball if he doesn't have the bat.

If you took that bat away from a baseball player, then there would be no way for them to play.

Many companies feel as though the sales reps need to pay for their tools. This is not a bad thing because if they pay for them, then they are going to use them.

If the company pays for them, chances are that they are probably not going to use them because it's just something they got during training and if I need it, I'll run out and grab it. They never do.

Whether they pay for them or explain what it is that they need, these are the tools for success, these are the tools that they need to succeed in their position, whether we physically hand the tools to them or mandate that they have them and teach them how to use them.

Having the right knowledge, training, and tools will set them up for success.

Empathy versus Sympathy

When you are in a leadership position, and someone comes and asks you for help, if you take it over and do it for them, they will continue to do that over and over again.

We got into the idea of empathy and sympathy earlier, and this is another way to look at the difference.

We still get the question every day, "I'm so busy because my sales reps come to me for everything."

Are you surprised? If you take care of this situation, they are going to continue to come back to you time and time again.

My favorite thing to do when someone comes and asks me, depending on what it is, is to say, "You go out, and you find the answer. If you cannot find the answer, come back, and I will help you."

I have been doing this for 20 years, and I still have yet for someone to come back to me. They always find the answer for themselves.

This will enable your team to understand that they can find other answers, and it also gives you the freedom of not always having to be there for the rescue. The team can't use a sales leader because they are too lazy to go find the answer themselves. Sales leaders feel like they always need to be the hero, but they don't need to be the hero.

It is very hard for a sales leader just like anyone, because we want to be seen as the best. Most of these sales leaders just don't know what being the best looks like.

If you go and see one of these leaders who truly gets it and knows what they are doing and how to do it, they are not answering questions all day, because their sales reps know the answers. They allow their sales reps to go find those answers for themselves.

Don't put the monkey on your back, as I wrote earlier. That sympathy response won't serve you in your business.

You are going to take their problem, and you are going to solve it for them. Now you have their burden, because they gave it to you.

Empathy is where they are going to come to you, and where you help them understand what is going on, then handing them back their problem for them to solve.

If You Can Be Misunderstood, You Will Be

There are times when you are going to give information, and sometimes that information is not easy to give, and you will just have to hit them right between the eyes.

If you dance around the problem, and you make it seem like everything will be okay, then they are not going to understand what just happened, and they are not going to understand the severity of the issue.

This is why, in this situation, we want them to understand what the issue is and what needs to be done. Don't dance around it.

In many cases, when we say 'The biggest ship is leadership', we want to make sure that the sales leaders know that the way that they give that information needs to be straightforward. They need to say, "This color has been discontinued. It is on this memo, don't be that rep that brings a contract in tomorrow with these colors on it, because you are going back, and you will get a change order for a different color."

Instead, a lot of these sales leaders will dance around it, and say, "So as you guys know, the manufacturer did this and that, and so now this color is just no longer available. So make sure that your customers know about it."

This is all they say, and you would think it would be straightforward, but it is not. The salesmen come back with that color and you say, "That color was discontinued. We went through that this morning."

They say, "Yeah, but the customer really wants this color. They have got it somewhere. You can deal with that, right? Can you just try to find the color? Can you help me out?"

In these circumstances, the sales rep is going to start selling the sales leader more than they sell the homeowner. That clarity needs to be very crisp, clear, and precise.

The easiest way to make sure that there is no misunderstanding is to make sure that anything that needs to be understood should be in writing.

I wish there was a nice way to say this, but again, when you are giving information, you have to hit them right between the eyes with it. Never leave room for different interpretations of what you are saying.

Lifelines

Whether it is the sales leader, the production leader, or maybe even the owner, what are all the ways that they can get information when they are with a customer? What do they do when a customer calls them and needs information? What are the sales rep's lifelines?

The sales rep needs to make sure that they are not making people upset because they are going to be less likely to get an answer when they need it. They need to have those lifelines when the customer needs help. Sometimes it is the group text, or in the intranet that many organizations have so that they can talk back and forth. It's a good idea to have a resource center at their fingertips with spec sheets, mins and max numbers, field guides, warranties, company insurance docs, reference sheets, and anything else you feel they will need in the field.

Other lifelines could be asking for help from the other leaders or owners. Anyone that would know that answer should be available or try to be available. The sales rep needs to know that.

If not, perhaps you get new sales reps, ask them why they didn't call the admin. They will say, "I don't know who the admin is, I don't have their information."

Make sure that they have that information available to them.

It would also be good to know when everyone is available, whether it is at a different time of the day, or if they are only available at certain times.

Sales leaders should be available too, and should not be turning off their phones. If a sales leader feels like they should be able to turn off their phones at certain points, they shouldn't be a sales leader. The sales leader made a commitment when they accepted the job.

Another option is to have coaches inside of the team. When you have larger teams, you can employ some of your more knowledgeable sales reps to answer questions also. You may ask that everyone call them before they call you. Be careful calling these individuals leaders or supervisors. Have you heard that titles are free? That is completely false. Call someone a leader and watch their entire demeanor change. This is why we call them coaches.

No one can win by themselves. No one can go out there and dominate the industry by themselves. This is all a team, and we need to support each other and make sure that we all have what we need to succeed. They say that raising a child takes a village, and taking care of a sales rep sometimes can take a village too.

If you do your job, and you grease the wheels correctly, there is no way that you can fail. Even in a poor economy, your team should be successful and be able to stay positive.

A gauge for understanding whether you are greasing the wheels or not is the culture inside your organization or your team.

If you have a very negative culture or a negative feel, that is because of you, the sales leader.

You didn't do your job to grease the wheels that needed to be greased.

Chapter 6

FORECASTING: THE CRYSTAL BALL

Looking at trends in business is like looking into a crystal ball. It will predict what will happen, and you will know the next steps to take to get the outcome that you want.

Everybody says that they know their numbers, but unfortunately, most people do not. Most don't know what number they should be focused on.

You cannot just look at your year and say, "We usually have a high June and a high March." You cannot look at that and just say those are your big months. What do you do in the other months?

You have to have an educated look at every single month. There is a book called 'Psycho-Cybernetics' by Maxwell Maltz, he talks about having the entire field in front of you and working your way back from the result that you want in the end. If you make the decision of what your year needs to look like, we can easily work everything back to educated monthly numbers using your current KPIs.

We work backward. We know what we want to end up with at the end of the year. Every great achievement was achieved by looking at the end result and working your way back.

Tiger Woods pictures the ball in the hole, and then he brings the ball back and goes into his backswing position. That is how a lot of these things are done. We picture the end result in our minds first, then work our way back.

If we start with the fact that we want to sell $10 million, $20 million, or $100 million, then we should look at every month and see what every month has to look like based on our experience, which is our trend.

If you have that available, we take four years, and then we average that out so that we have a perfect bell curve over time. Then, from there, we start to run our numbers.

Most people do not even know what a bell curve is, let alone what their bell curve is. They could probably tell me what months are typically high for them, but they could not tell me what percentage of the total revenue goal that is. They can say June is a big month, which tells me absolutely nothing.

The problem is, they don't know what they don't know about what the trend is or what their bell curve is until we show them on a screen. When we show them the concept for the first time, they realize, "Wow, man, if I just knew what ours was, do you know what I could do?"

Yeah, I know exactly what you can do. We have put this concept into many of the largest organizations in the country.

The process of the crystal ball lays out the yellow brick road for people in sales. If you are walking and everything is foggy, and you have no idea if the road is going to go left or right, the crystal ball clears out the fog. Everything is shown to them. All they need to do is know exactly what they are supposed to do.

This is like getting a lottery ticket number and giving them the numbers to win that lottery. All they have to do is play these numbers, and they can win the lottery. That is what we are doing.

Once we have their bell curve, we can work out everything, all the way back to the raw lead and the number of raw leads they need to come in through the front door to achieve that goal each month. This can be nothing more than saying, "Let's inform and push our marketing people."

This is laying the entire groundwork out. If you are following a path, and it is so foggy out that you cannot see where you are going, you start to slow down because you wonder if you are going to walk off the path and hit a tree.

You have no idea when the road is going to go left, when it is going to go right, or what is going to happen. Then, once we learn the bell curve, it is like the fog just disappears and everything sits out in front of you. Not only that but now you also have a view over the top. Not only are you walking, but you can see the map of where you are going.

If you use the crystal ball, you will get a clear understanding of how to achieve the goal that you have set for yourself. Most people that we encounter say, “We want to sell 50 million.”

When we ask them how they intend to do that, their answer is typically, “We’re going to work harder than we did last year.”

I don’t even know what kind of answer that is. They have no idea what they are doing, but for us, once we lay it out, we know exactly how many raw leads we need, and we know exactly how many appointments those raw leads will turn into based on our current conversion ratio. So we are giving them the roadmap to success and making it easy.

They also have to put in the work and know what they are working towards. The marketing department should know exactly how many leads they need. Before, they were just supposed to deliver as many leads as they could. If you work as hard as you can and get as many leads as you can get, you will never hit your goal. But, if you give them a number, they will hit it because they know what it takes to hit that specific number.

When we are working with an organization, they are usually surprised when we tell them how many leads they actually need. That is the most important number. We do not look at it and say, "You really need to be at this close rate, and you need to be at this conversation rate." We look at their current standings.

Some of these are bad, but we still look at their current standings, and they are going to look at their raw leads and say, "There's no way I could ever get that many." Well, with the way that they sell and the way that they market, they are not, but with coaching and strategy they can lay out the plan to raise that close rate, average sale, and lead conversion rate. Using those KPIs like dials on a stereo, if you move one or all of them, the number of needed leads will go down. So what can you do to affect the success of the sales team to move those dials? What can the marketing department and phone department do to increase their success? Everyone knowing the number and working together will enable the company to hit these goals.

There is a company in Cincinnati where we knew exactly how many raw leads we needed to come in, and we budgeted, based on a 10% marketing cost, exactly how big our marketing spend needed to be.

We devised a plan through our marketing department to use that marketing spend to get a certain number of raw leads. Our conversion rate is the ratio of our raw leads to appointments. If we convert 75% of all raw leads to appointments, now I know how many appointments we will get. If I knew that we closed at 40%, meaning that from all the appointments we ran, we closed 40% of those deals, and I know the average sale amount, then now I know how many sales I need. This tells me exactly what I need to get to that specific goal.

Again, we work backward.

When I say we work backward, it is by asking how much you want to sell and then seeing what our bell curve looks like, which then tells me what every month is. Then I find out what our average sales amount is. The average sale means the average dollar amount of every sale. Let's say sales average $15,000. So for example, if we take a $100,000 goal, and divide it by $15,000, this will tell me how many deals I need that month (6.6 rounded to 7). If our close rate is 40%, we are going to take the number of deals each month and divide by .4 (17.5 rounded to 18 appointments). This will give us the number of appointments that we need per month.

If we use those figures and work our way back, then that crystal ball will tell us what we need every month, not just what we need for the year divided by twelve. What most companies do is divide by twelve, and then they start to work their numbers from there, and then they are upset at the end because they are nowhere near their goal. This is because they missed a major piece, which is the bell curve.

If the companies are new and do not have four years of data, we look at other companies. We cannot tell them what companies we look at, but we tell them that we have other companies in the area or in that demographic similar to theirs. We then use those bell curves until we get theirs.

If I just had one year, it would at least give me a bell curve. It may not be the best bell curve, but as we go year after year, it gets better and more precise as we go along.

You're not done yet. Now that you have the company's numbers mapped out. How are you going to get your sales reps to hit these numbers? We do the same math for them. Instead of asking them for their yearly number goal, I want to know how much income they want this year. Then ask them what number would change their life? This will be their BHAG. Using the same math, you will be able to give each individual sales rep their specific monthly numbers to hit their goals. It's important to break down the sales reps numbers into weekly also. Remember, this is a game of inches, the reps inches are their days and weeks.

Picture yourself running down a path. This path is pretty curvy, and filled with fog to the point that you cannot see more than five feet in front of your face. You are scared, so you slow down.

In this scenario, you would wish that you could lift the fog and know exactly where you were going and where every turn was. That is what I hope this chapter can do for you.

Right now, you might be going through each individual month, and you never really know how much you are going to sell, or even what you are supposed to sell. Even worse, you may not know how to do it.

You might be thinking, 'I know how to do it, I just have to work harder', but that is not an answer. It is more scientific than that.

You need to understand that what you are doing right now is running through a room with the lights off. If you were to run at full speed, you would run right into the wall. But I can turn on the lights for you. I can show you where all the exits are, and light the way forward.

This is your crystal ball. It is going to show you your future and how to get there.

There is anxiety among all sales leaders. We are forced to succeed, and the problem with most sales leaders is that the only way that we succeed is if we push our sales reps harder. We do not even know where we are pushing them. We are hoping that we can raise their close rate, raise their average sale, and raise their NSLI (Net Sales Per Lead Issued), but we really have no idea what level we have to raise it to in order to be successful. All they know is they need to be better, that means very little.

If they just had that crystal ball, if they had all the numbers sitting in front of them, then they could say, "If your sales reps would just hit this number, then you would be successful this month. Then next month, this is what you need." We need to be working on next month while we are working on and closing out this month. Again, we have our team. Our team is the marketing team, the phone team, and the sales team, and everyone has to be on the same page.

This takes the anxiety away, which basically is the fear of the unknown. I am sure that you have some instances of this where you get so anxiety-ridden because you do not know what is coming next.

Maybe your schedule is not completely mapped out, or you do not know how something is going to work out. We all get there.

Imagine if all of this fell in your lap, and it was a complete path of what to do. Like being told, "If you just did this, then all the other things would be easy," or "If you just did this, then this would happen." That is what we are doing. We are taking the anxiety and the guesswork away of what you should do. I may be making your position boring as a sales leader because I am telling you what you lack and what you should put into place, and all you would need to do is walk the path.

I think all sales leaders would welcome boredom. It is one extreme or the other. Either I am anxiety-ridden because I have to hit a certain number and don't know exactly how to hit it, or it is boring because I know how to hit it and I know that I am going to hit it because the team knows what numbers to hit. Or you are in an organization that doesn't care as long as you do your job.

Unfortunately, there are such organizations out there because they don't know any better. They put their sales leader out, and they say, "Do your best," then they wonder why they are not successful. They wonder why they struggle, and wonder why it is not as easy. They look at other owners and think, 'Why is it that guy can go play golf, or he's on vacation all the time, and his business runs without him.' It is because he has the right people in place and they have a complete road map. He can walk away and understand that as long as they follow that roadmap, success will come.

Knowing What You Want

It is not only the number that matters, it is also what the organization would look like when we hit that number. What can we do? As an organization, if we hit our conservative goal, what is the organization going to look like, and what can we do as an organization if we hit the BHAG?

We have to see what that is. Again, there has to be a feeling, and there has to be some excitement there, like, 'I must hit this commitment.' What would reaching this commitment mean for the company? What would it mean for you as a leader?

Hitting this commitment may even make you feel like a success. There is a difference between hitting the commitment and you feeling like you are a success.

But what if you don't hit the commitment? What does that feel like?

This is the opposite of making you feel like you are a success, right? What is that?

Nobody wants to talk about that. Nobody wants to be a failure. It's not about failing unless you and your team failed to do the activities required to win. We learn when we come up short of our commitment.

We talk about that when we talk about the crystal ball. We explain it just like that. We say, "You either hit it and you are a success, or you don't hit it, and you learn."

We want them to realize that if you're going for $10 million, and you hit $9.5 million, What caused us to come up short? Be careful not to make excuses to justify your shortcomings. Excuses make you feel better and ensure you will fail again.

People say that coming in second place means that you are just the first loser. You want to win. If you had the roadmap in front of you to win, why not follow it?

The conservative goal is your budget goal. That is what you budget your marketing on, and that is what you budget all your sales on. This is the thing that you have to hit as a sales leader. I like to say that is what you hit to keep your job, and that is usually the only number most people know. What is even worse is that they don't even know why. The number is just there because that is something that they would sure like to hit one day. There is no mathematical reason for that goal.

If they want to increase their goals or their sales, they want to double. We say that you should double up to $10 million (depending on your trade). Then, from there, it is not a bad idea to go up 10% to 30% per year. That is good growth.

Your BHAG is the Jim Collins concept that we've been mentioning throughout, the 'big, hairy, audacious goal'. It is a stretch goal. It is that goal that is just out of reach, and you don't even know how you are really going to hit it. When we talk to sales reps, we ask them, "What would change your life? What would change your family's lifestyle?"

It is funny how many times it is a brand-new concept for people. Every time I say, "It's a big, hairy, audacious goal," they will laugh, and I will realize that they have never heard that before. It is something that bigger companies discuss during their annual meetings.

Let's say it again for the people in the back. You need to know what your conservative goal is so that you know exactly what you have to hit. You want to know what that BHAG is because that is what you need to be reaching for. The reason why you want to reach for that BHAG is because if you only had that conservative goal and mapped everything out for that conservative goal, then you probably wouldn't hit it. You may even feel okay about not hitting that target.

If you map it out for that BHAG and go after that BHAG, you will at least hit your conservative goal, if not halfway to actually hitting your BHAG.

Most of our clients this year went past their BHAG because we mapped it out for them. When they had the numbers in front of them, they saw just how easy it was to hit them.

Knowing Your Current KPIs

You have to be very true to yourself when you look at your KPIs.

This is not locker room talk where you go into the conventions and say a KPI that is double what you are actually doing. If you really want to be true to yourself, this is the time to do it. If your close rate is 20.5%, it should be rounded down to 20%. The reason is that the numbers that you have to hit are based on those KPIs.

These KPIs, except for the conversion ratio, are very widely used. The average sale and the close rate are very widely used. Unfortunately, that conversion ratio is not widely used. Usually, when we ask people what that is, they don't know, and they have no idea. They will even tell you, "We don't even track our raw leads," which is crazy to me.

I tell my clients that if I could even track how many times my guys used the bathroom, I would. We want to know everything.

The current close rate is the probability of closing the deal and closing the job. They get that by taking their appointments and their closed jobs and coming up with the percentage. They will come up with what the percentage of their qualified appointments is to the closed sales.

Whether it is over a month, a quarter, or over a year, you must know what the average size deal is. Some will be $5,000, depending on what they are selling, and some will be as much as $50,000. That could be their average sale.

We want to know their average sales so that we can know how many sales they need. That is how we figure it out. We will divide their total annual or monthly revenue by their average sale amount.

The conversion rate is the percentage of raw leads that lead to qualified appointments. If their phone room only converts 20%, that means that for all the raw leads that come in through all their lead sources, they were able to convert 20% of those leads into actual appointments. This also means that 80% are still sitting in their database, needing to be booked.

The conversion rate is important because it tells them the success of their phone room or phone person. It also helps them to realize how good that lead source is or to understand the lead source. There are some lead sources that we expect to have a 20% conversion rate. There are some lead sources that we expect to have an 80%-90% conversion rate. So with all of them together, it gives us our actual conversion ratio.

If you look at these three and look at them as dials, some dials are easier to turn than others, so the average sale will not be as easily turned as a conversion ratio or a close rate. If we just work with the sales team and work to close more deals, then that dial is a little easier to turn up, and we just need to call that conversion ratio twice as often. But for that average sale, we have to add products or services, raise prices, or sell higher systems. This might bring our close rate down if we don't work with our team on their closing process. These are all plates that we as leaders keep spinning.

We may have to crank them up. When we move a close rate, an average sale, or that conversion ratio, that is 400 raw leads that I am supposed to be getting, and it may go down to 310. Now I only need 310 leads because I was able to turn all three dials.

Knowing their KPIs will allow them to understand their level of performance, it will tell them where they need help, and will also let them know what the numbers need to be, whether they are good or bad. It will let them know how many raw leads, how many appointments, and how many sales they need.

Another KPI that you should watch is your "Sit/ Demo Rate," which is the percentage of appointments we actually give a demo and leave a price with the prospect. Depending on your other numbers, this could show you a weak sales rep, poor phone rep, or poor procedures for your people to follow.

Most retail organizations watch their NSLI (Net Sales Per Lead Issued). Many call this your Slugging Average. This number has your Close Rate, Average Sale and Profitability all wrapped up in one number. Once this number drops, you use the other KPIs to drill down and find out what's going on.

The number most organizations neglect to add to their KPIs is "Profit." When looking at all of the other indicators of success, if you don't monitor the profit, the other numbers clearly don't matter. When going into several large sales organizations of over $100M+ in yearly revenue, you would think they have all the systems and ability to monitor everything including how many times an individual goes to the bathroom if needed. We noticed great conversion rates and closing. Everything seemed to look really good, until I noticed that they didn't have the individual average profit KPIs listed. When pulling the profit numbers, we noticed that several of their top performers, based on Close Rate and NSLI, had very little to no profit.

Breaking Down the Number

As I mentioned in a previous chapter, the bell curve is the trend.

If you look at a flow graph, you can see January, February, March, and April, and you can see how it flows through. There is a lot that it will tell you, like when you are going to need more sales reps.

Some months are bad and some are good. The problem is that if you do not know exactly what that means, then knowing that some months are good, and some months are bad tells you absolutely nothing.

If I were to tell you that January is 4.72% of your total goal, now we are getting somewhere, because I can do the math. If I were to tell you that February is 10.85% of your total goal, and that is a good month, then that would tell you something.

For example, you would know if June is better or less than March because it's 13.5% of your total goal. This is the level of detail that we get it into.

For the marketing curve, we need to know what our spending needs to be. In October of every year, we look at our budgets for the next year, and we look at the fact that certain months are high, and we need to know why they are high.

If they are high because of a home show, then we do not need to pump the marketing because of that. If other months are high because it is a high month, then that is when people are buying. Let's push the marketing dollars into those months because we should push our peaks and hide our valleys, which means that we save on the valleys.

I am not going to spend more money to bring it out of the hole if we know that it is going to go down whether I spend more or not.

The sales leader needs to be aware of the marketing curve, and they need to share it with the marketing people. A lot of times, the marketing people are a third party, maybe a marketing boutique or marketing company, and they need to share the trend with them.

If we know that March is a huge month, that means that in February we need to push the money. If you push it in March, it is done. You are pushing March to get April going. We always start a month earlier, if not a little bit sooner, depending on the time of year.

Showing the marketing people our bell curve allows them to understand what the lead time is. If I spend $100,000, at what point will those leads come in? Will they come in immediately? On some sources, they will. On TV? No, not so much. Again, that helps the marketing people know when to push the marketing and when to pull back.

The sales curve is what the sales leader forecasts from what is their monthly figure. The appointment curve is what the phone room leader watches, and they then look at their bell curve. You can do everything off of the sales curve, or you can do it based on each curve, which would be more precise.

If you had every one of these, and you had separate numbers for when the leads came in, when the calls were booked, and when the sales were made, those all would be a little different, but yet you would still see the trend.

If you look at them, and you overlap how the marketing affects the phones and how the phones affect the sales, it looks like one hump, another hump, and another hump because it all happens right after each other.

The production curve is just a little bit different, but this is when we know when we need to ramp up on installers or book installs differently. Most people are so far behind, and they have these big lead times, that they cannot seem to get these jobs installed, and they are three months out.

This is simply poor planning, and they did not ramp up their production team because production and sales were not talking. "We're going to have a huge month next month. Are you ready for it?" said no sales leader ever, because they do not talk to the production leader very often.

This does affect sales because if they tell the homeowner, "We're six months behind," that is going to be a really hard sale. If you want your back door replaced, and I told you that we could not get it to you for six months, you will probably look for somebody who can do it sooner.

This affects sales in many ways.

Most people understand the number of sales and appointments, and they also understand the number of leads. The problem is that they do not understand that leads are the most important number. If all of your KPIs are correct, those other numbers will take care of themselves.

If you have a 45% close rate, then you know how much you are going to get based on that 45% close rate. If you are supposed to have 400 leads, and you do not deliver 400 leads, you will never hit those numbers of sales. It is not going to work, so leads are the most important number.

What Do You Do With the Numbers?

Once we have the numbers, that is when we use the dials.

This is when we start to look at the KPIs, and we start with the easy ones first. As a sales leader, I am going to take it upon myself to look at the close rate first, and understand what my gaps inside that close rate are. To raise your close rate, you can do this in several ways. For the individual sales reps, training, verification, and accountability is how this is done. Make sure they are trained correctly and they have mastered the process laid out in your Key Competency List. These are the activities we manage as leaders. Then we verify that they use the process correctly in the house. This is done with consistent ride-alongs throughout the month. Then hold them accountable for the results. If you provide company generated appointments to your reps, you have a responsibility to give your team qualified appointments before you have the right to hold them accountable to the results.

To increase your close rate as a team, you need to look at your whole team objectively so that you can see each member of the team for their performance, contributions and numbers and not the person. I know this can be hard when we want to operate from a place of servant leadership, however, there is a time that we must look at the whole picture and look for the anchors holding us down.

As a professional sports team, there are players we all like but they just aren't performing to the level needed to stay on the team. So find those players and allow them to be successful elsewhere. This is assuming you have already retrained them to bring their potential for success up. Once you eliminate those that are dragging your close rate down, you will see a big boost in your KPIs. This also makes room for a new champion to join the team.

The next dial you can turn is your average sale. Increasing the average sale is done by increasing your price, offering additional products or services, or upgrading them to the next system. This is simple but requires training and accountability also so that you don't sacrifice close rate or profit.

Once you have your numbers, it is important to talk to the other departments, but the other departments don't talk, and this is a huge problem in most organizations. The sales leader is working with me, and they know the numbers. But the problem is that they won't take it down the hallway and show the marketing guy and say, "Hey, did you know that I needed 450 leads?"

The marketing guy says, "That is the first time I've ever seen that."

Again, all the marketing person felt was, 'We seem to be doing well. The marketing is converting, and we had 20 leads last week', but what he does not know is that 20 leads are not even going to get us anywhere close to our goal.

They need to know their breakdowns based on the numbers. They need to know that if they need 450 leads, they are going to do it. Everyone needs to know their numbers and be held accountable for them once they commit to hitting it. Everyone has to have their expectations. We know that we succeed and fail based on these numbers, so they have to be vocal.

I will also tell you that there are a lot of people who are let go because of these numbers. If someone comes in and says, “I can’t hit those numbers,” there are a lot of people that will be let go, because if you cannot hit them, I will find someone who can. That is a hard reality to face.

Some people will tell you, “I can do that,” knowing that they can’t and have no idea how they are going to do it. This is why we work as a team, and we are going to help each other out. If you feel that you don’t know how you are going to do that, let me know, because I want to know now, not at the end of the month. We are a team and we can work through this as a team.

As a sales leader, I have two people in front of me who have to hit their goals before I can even look at hitting my goals. If the marketing person and the phone room do not hit their goals, I won’t even come near mine, and I can’t use that as an excuse. Just like the sports coach, who is always in the newspaper, the fact that I didn’t hit the sales goal, I am the one that is going to be in front of the owner. You don’t see the marketing person or the phone person in trouble because I couldn’t hit my goal, that is for sure.

The sales leader has to sit there, grin, and bear it, knowing that it may not completely be their fault, but it is because they didn't share the needed numbers and didn't hold the other two people accountable. It is the sales leader's position to make sure that everybody knows where they stand based on the numbers that are needed.

You can either walk the mapped-out, yellow brick road, or you can sit there and continue to walk through the fog.

Ultimately, that is up to you. What is even worse is that most will continue to walk through the fog because it is easier than trying to map out the numbers. There is a certain number of you that will always be walking through the fog. If you were to just map out your numbers and do it right, everything would be so much easier. But you still will not do it.

For whatever reason, people will read through a book and think it is cool, or they will watch us talk on stage and think it's cool, but they won't do the stuff.

It is just a lazy factor. They know what they are supposed to do, but they just won't do it.

For the people who do it, they will find out how easy success is.

Take the time and slow down.

Take the time to put the numbers on paper.

Take the time to map out your success and look at it as a complete roadmap.

Once you find those numbers, be diligent in how you are going to follow this roadmap.

It is going to be hard when you look at it.

I don't want you to alter that number for your goals, if you just raised your close rate or if you just worked on your phone team to increase your conversion ratio, then you will see the numbers that you need to hit for everything but the sale.

The only way that you are going to get your number of sold jobs down is to raise your average sale. If you just raised your conversion ratio or your closing rate, you might find that the number of raw leads you need gets cut to a manageable level. Things get easier if you just become more efficient.

If you don't know what to work on to make yourself more efficient, you are not going to work on anything, and you are still the same person who says, "We just need to get better."

Chapter 7

BUILDING BLOCKS: SALES TEAM KEY COMPETENCIES

There is a great deal that goes into training new talent. So much, in fact, that you will forget things.

You are going to forget something like financing, or you are going to forget some of the closes. If you do not have it completely laid out and have a checklist of everything that needs to be trained and everything that must be mastered, then it won't be complete.

It is like building a car from a kit, finding out that after you're done, you have parts left over.

You think, 'Hopefully it runs. I got half the parts still sitting on the floor, but it looks like a car.'

That is the problem. We want to make sure that while we are going through training, everything has been checked off. Not just checked off, but mastered too.

When we look at building blocks, we have the foundation, which is the training itself. We have to go through basic training. All the basics that the sales rep should learn are the basis of it. We then put everything on top so that while we build the sales rep and the sales team, those are all pieces and parts of the building blocks.

In the end, you will have a sales team that dominates. You will have a sales team that all sings the same song and all works together.

The team that does not have the building blocks is something we often witness. These are people that we see all day long.

They are in business, they struggle to get past the point of $5-10 million, and it is all because they are just going through the motions. They have no purpose for what they do daily. They go through the motions, they give the proposal, and then they cross their fingers that they will get called back.

There is no selling system, and there is no training system. All of the sales reps do something different. So when they are in the sales meeting, no one knows what to talk about, and it is chaos. This typically will not let them go past $10 million, if even $5 million, depending on the trade, but they are not going to go past a certain point.

This is what we call the struggle point. They are going to go and hit their heads on this ceiling.

They are going to struggle to get past this because they don't know what they don't know.

Or they do know what they don't know, and they don't know what to do about it.

With many of the companies that we deal with, when we go in, we find out that they went out and hired a bunch of sales reps, and each of them does something different.

They don't have a training process, and they don't know what they are supposed to do other than sell the job.

They whine and complain that they cannot seem to make it past a certain point.

For example, they are selling at a 17% to 20% close rate, and they cannot seem to get past that. There is no process, there is nothing there other than a bunch of representatives who know how to fill out a form and get something into production if it sells. More of an order taker culture.

They are operating on luck.

When they have the building blocks, they will have all the training, and the knowledge, and they follow the process. When that lead comes in, they know that they have to call within a certain period of time, typically 5 minutes. They know what it takes to qualify that appointment to make sure that the sales rep has an opportunity to close that job. Then, they put it on the calendar within the next three days because they know if they go over those three days it is most likely going to be canceled because another company has already sold it.

They are going to make the appointment within those three days, and then when that sales rep goes out, he has a process that he is going to follow to the tee. He is going to go through the entry and warm up, he is going to go through his survey/fact finding process, he is going to go do the walk around, get into the inspection, and get his pictures and his videos.

When he comes back to the table, he is going to share a presentation with the homeowner that will separate them from everybody else. He will then go through a price presentation and will be ready to deal with any stalls, excuses, or objections that the homeowner might give after they have given the price.

The difference between the two is that one does not have a system, and they work on hopes and prayers, while the other one has a system, and they are successful because everything is laid out.

Neither one of them will close 100% of the time. However, one will close at 20%. The other one will close at anywhere between 45% to 70%.

Winners and losers always have the same goal in mind. The problem is that the winners have a game plan. Everybody that shows up to the house has the same goal, which is to sell their solution. Only one of them has an actual game plan in mind.

The building blocks are the selling process, the training process, the key competencies, mindset, and knowing what gaps they need to be trained on if they aren't new.

For most sales leaders, all they know is what the result has to be. They know that by the end of the month, they need to sell $700,000, and they keep pushing their team like, "All right, guys, we've got to hit $700,000 this month. I've got to hit the $700,000." But they're not managing any of the activities. They're only focused on the end result.

If you were to manage the activities, then you are going to blow past the expected result. We have to manage the activities, not the results.

What is it that sales reps need to do to hit the result?

That is why we have to track the key competencies. And why you should run your 'power hour' each morning, where you find out what happened and then what was not followed, what they could have done better, or we cheer on when they win.

If you are going to build this 'building', these are all the things that have to go into the entire sales management model. Not one thing works by itself. All the things that I wrote about work together. These are the building blocks.

This is about how you manage your team and their expectations. Now that we have built the team, we have built the expectations, and we are going to understand how to train that team, how we are going to hold them accountable? All of this will lead you to be the sales leader that you have wanted to be since you started reading this book.

It is time to start building.

The Selling System

If people already have a sales system, they should know it. The problem is that most of their sales reps do not know about it.

The selling system is anywhere between six and ten steps, depending on the organization. The one that we teach is your entry and warm-up, and then you are going to ask surface level questions with the homeowner. It is a process of them knowing what they are supposed to do while they are going through the process with the homeowner, and this doesn't change. When they pick a selling process or selling system, it should be written in stone in their organization. Every sales rep should know it cold, but they usually don't.

Why do we use step selling systems? The only reason is to make sure you have a system that works for all of your current and future team members. Many of the best sales professionals around the world started with a sales process and have graduated to more of a solutions based process that allows for purpose driven questioning systems that are best suited for advanced and more comfortable sales professionals. We teach these also when we feel someone is ready.

When they go in, they have to know the sales process so well they can't get it wrong. If you have ever bought from a true sales professional, They know their process very well. They are going to make a friend, and they are going to make sure that the prospects are following along depending on their personality style.

They will ask you a little bit about your family, 'What do you do for a living? What is it that you like to do?' This allows the sales professional to start the conversation outside of the solution they are selling.

You get the sense that they are interested in you. This is great but truly, what they are trying to do is get you to talk and build rapport with you. Once they get that rapport, they move on to explaining what is going to happen today. Then, they are going to go into a survey/situational questions. That survey is to get them to tell you how they are sold without asking them that.

There is a whole process that we go through, and you have no idea what is going on behind the scenes. This is why we have a sales process. By the time we are ready to ask you for the deal, this solution will seem so easy to afford, the fact that we are $4,000 more than our competitor won't matter due to the value we are going to provide.

Every question that they ask you has a purpose behind it. We are just getting all this information from you so that when we ask you to buy, we are already armed with everything we need to close the deal.

Every sales rep is supposed to know this. Sales reps who truly do their job care about the homeowner. When I speak, I will tell everybody in the audience, "I want you to do something for me. Get a piece of paper out. I want you to write down all the companies in your area that would screw over the homeowner. It should not take you but ten seconds to write ten names."

They all laugh because it is true. They know them all by heart, and they will write them all down.

Then I will say, "So now I want you to think of your last customer."

I will pick someone, and they're going to say, "Bob and Mary are an older couple," and they will tell me everything about what he does, what she does, and what they really need and why. They are giving me a whole backstory.

I ask, "You really like these people, right? These people feed your lifestyle. Am I right? They enable you to have that lifestyle, correct?"

They will say, "Yeah."

Your job is to make sure that they do not do business with anybody on that page. We save people, we don't sell them. All of a sudden, they realize we save people, we don't sell them.

Their entire purpose for being there suddenly changes. What comes out of them when they are explaining the process to people like Bob and Mary sounds different. This becomes an emotional sale, not just for them but for us. That is why we have changed the model. We might be the highest price, but we are also going to still be in business when you need us.

This is not a race to the bottom, we are not trying to be the cheapest, we just want to be the best.

When we look at the building blocks, it is everything that we are doing to save the homeowner, not sell them. But what is the only way that we can ensure that we get the opportunity to save them? Or what is the only way we can keep them from doing business with those other people?

It is to close them.

Everything that we do, like the people I choose, the players on my team, how I train them, how I hold them accountable, and how I book the appointments, all goes into enabling us to save the homeowner, not sell them. It's the selling culture that we build.

If I can make this a conversation, then it truly is in the homeowner's best interest. If it is nothing but a script, then the sales rep does not even know what they are talking about. They are just regurgitating what they are supposed to say. Knowing why you say it and the problems that you are solving brings a totally different tone and emotion to the meeting, making it easier to sell the product or service.

If you and I were to talk, and I was to sell you windows, baths or roofing, at the end of it, you would think, 'Oh my gosh, Chuck is so nice. He seems so knowledgeable.' I put myself into a perception of being an expert and not a sales rep. It's about solving a problem and not selling a product.

What you don't know is that I went through an entire process with you. You felt like it was just a simple conversation that you and I had, and I just happened to be knowledgeable about the problem that you have, and was able to offer an easy to understand solution. That is a sales professional.

If at the end, you felt like I just interrogated you, that I threw you a bunch of one-liners, and at the end, I asked you to buy, and you just didn't feel all that comfortable, then that is someone who just learned a bunch of scripts and does not know well enough to make it a conversation.

The Training Process

Training for knowledge and mastery are two different things.

The reason why we train is to make sure that the people that we hire can do the job the way that we need them to do the job. A lot of them come in, and they know it, and we could probably just hand them our contracts and say good luck, but we want everybody singing the same song and doing the same thing.

If everyone sells the same way, then we can all, as a team, get better. If everyone sells a different way, then there is nothing you can ever do to make your team better because everyone does something different. You cannot work together. It would be impossible to have a productive sales meeting.

If you had a bunch of contractors working on a house, but they all built the house differently, the house would fall apart. But if everyone had the same plans, the same direction, and the same training, and the house was going to be built the same way that it is put on that piece of paper, then we are building a strong house that will last.

We are training everyone the same way. We are getting them to close the same way so that when we come in every week during the sales meeting when we are training on the close, then we know that all 20 people are doing the same close. When we are going through it, I am not just talking to two guys because they are the only ones that do it this way. Everybody must do it the same way.

Sales are by no means like riding a bike. If you stop training for a few weeks, you will start to close your own way again, you will start to forget things. The same thing is true when we are talking about how the homeowner trains the reps. If you are not going to train your rep, the homeowner will. What that means is that you go in, you train them, and you think that your job is done, but they forget to get into the attic, they forget to get into the crawl space, or they forget to get into the access panel, and the homeowner does the worst thing they can do, they buy.

All of a sudden, Your sales rep thinks, 'Well, I don't need to do that anymore. They bought it, and I didn't get into the attic, so I don't have to do that.'

Before you know it, you are not doing it any differently from any of the other contractors that come out, but you are still more expensive. You will start to wonder why your close rate goes down. You start to wonder why your price is higher than everybody else's, and you are not closing. This is typically when reps go back and tell leadership they are too expensive.

This is why we train, but we also verify. We either verify through recording, or we do all of the above, and we verify through ride-alongs, to make sure that the sales team is actually doing what needs to be done in the house and knows why their close rate is the way it is.

To sum that up, we train so that everybody sings the same song and that they all do it the same way. You are going to get people who will tell you that it is like building robots.

If I could build robots, I would. We have to look at what wins most of the time, not what people think the best way of doing it for them is. We do what is best, and the best way to do it for the team.

We are looking for consistency. People do not understand why a lot of companies are so good and grow so quickly, but it is because of consistency. This process is more consistent than others.

Some people say, "I sell this way because that is the best way for me." But that is not the best way for the company, so you might need to move on or buy into this process. Do you allow your production staff to install any way they like? No! So why would you allow your sales team to sell any way they would like? The results would be the same, bad installs and no sales.

Key Competencies

The key competencies are a list of everything that people need to know. The key competencies for a sales rep consists of everything they do to prepare for the appointment, the entry and warm up, and everything that happens inside that entry and warm up.

It is not a descriptive thing like handing them a script. It is understanding things like where they parked, how long before they got out of the vehicle, if there was any eye contact, and thanking them for inviting them out.

When we are training, I know that I will not miss anything because there is a list of everything that they must know, and I am going to grade them on everything. Whether I am training them or riding with them to verify that they are still doing everything, this is how we verify that they are very well-trained and that they are doing their job in the house.

This is not something that we do just once. We verify certain parts and pieces weekly, but it has to be done at least monthly to make sure that everybody is doing it the way that you are asking them to do it.

Something as simple as making a list of what you are supposed to do is instantly groundbreaking. We make the list, and we want to verify that this is what they are doing, but yet, when we are done with training, we know that they have mastered everything on that list.

This can be rated from one to five. Five means that they have mastered it, and you are not going to have a whole list of fives. You would like to say that they are all fives, but if you are honest with yourself and with your team, then you know that maybe they are not good at the presentation, but they are good at the close. They may be still trying to figure out the ventilation, or maybe it is how they are going to verify their measurements. We always have our finger on the pulse of each individual and where they are in their training.

Managing By Activities

We manage our team to make sure that they are doing their job, and that they do it consistently every single time. This way, at the end of the month, we know that we are going to hit the goal we are aiming for.

Every action has an equal and opposite reaction. If I run around the house, I will lose a certain amount of weight. If I do each one of these, then the chances of selling go up. When we manage the activities, the KPIs are also included.

Managing the activities could also be the sales leader's activities, like who you are going to put into the game or who you are sending out in the field. Those are also the activities that need to be managed. If I manage every individual rep, and they do what they are supposed to be doing, then their results will be there. You have the sales leader's results, which is the team's goal, and each individual rep has their own result.

How do we manage their activities?

Their activities are making sure they show up on time, making sure that when they get there, they are parking on the street, and that they get out of their car within 30 seconds. They should get out and smile at the house because they know that the digital doorbell is watching them. And they have to walk with purpose.

When they knock on the door, and when that door opens up, they should know what to say. They are going to ask if it is okay where they parked, and then they are going to put their surgical booties on so that they don't track anything from the outside in.

These are all the things that they need to do so the sales rep is successful. It is then about how they finish the job and how they follow-up with the homeowner. Everything the sales rep is supposed to do makes them successful and allows them to hit their goal.

Some of their activities are prospecting, and a lot of sales reps have to do their own prospecting. That is making the needed call, sending out text messages, doing their videos for social media, or knocking on doors and knowing what to say when that door opens up. Prospecting is just as important as selling. When they are done selling, they should 'clover leaf.'

Clover leafing is the act of going to the homes on either side of the house and the four homes in front of it to reach out to additional clients. This is something that every home services sales rep should be responsible for.

Power Hour

Accountability is key.

It's the accountability of knowing what happened the day or two days prior, depending on when you do your power hour.

This allows us to discuss the wins or the lessons learned. We never talk about 'no sales' as losses.

It is either celebrating the wins and talking about how they won, or talking about the lessons learned on the jobs that we did not sell. We get the team involved, this done as a group. You, as the leader, guide the team but they discuss the issues together. There should not be any negativity or tough talk in this hour.

I suggest doing this every morning while you are discussing the prior day. You are only going to want to make these discussions last an hour, depending on the prior day.

You can also bring in a topic, like maybe we want to discuss a certain product at the same time so that once we get done, we know that we have seven calls from yesterday, and we are going to talk about those. Then we are going to jump into a certain small sales or product topic.

Having power hours gives the team more training and accountability because they know that they are going to have to talk about this deal tomorrow, so they need to do their job in the house. If that appointment is something that is recorded, then they know that they can't just say, "Yeah, I did all that," because they have the recording of how that went.

Hopefully, the sales leader listened to it, and he could bring it up, and say, "Let's listen to how you went through this. I went ahead, and I keyed it up."

This way, they can go through how they went through that part of the appointment. It is not to make fun of them, it is so that we know how they did it and what we probably should do next time.

When it comes to giving tips and advice, it is a round table, and everyone is there. The sales leader is the moderator. It needs to be understood that we are going to give respect. We have all been there with this person who may have screwed up or could have done something different. If it is the same thing over and over, then there is going to be a problem.

For the most part, we discuss it, and then we want to make sure that they do not make that mistake again. We hold each other accountable, and we are a team.

Yesterday was just another quarter of the game, so we are going to come back and, as a team, we are going to talk about how we played the game yesterday. What is nice is that we get to go into today understanding what happened yesterday.

We are either going to extend that celebration, or we are not going to let the bloodshed continue into today.

Sales Meetings

Having an agenda is important, and that agenda has to be properly laid out. You have to go into each sales meeting with a topic, know what you are going to focus on, and train.

It is usually once a week for two hours. We will usually start a sales meeting at 9:00 am or 10:00 am, where power hours are usually from seven to eight in the morning. It will be before the day starts, so we are not disrupting anything.

Realize that those sales meetings, which are two hours long, are for the next seven days. The sales leader has two hours to make a big enough impact on the team to last until the next sales meeting. He or she is talking to his or her team throughout the week, but that sales meeting is really where the motivation, the training, and the mastery come in. That is the meat, and that is the vortex of the next week.

You will also have one-on-ones. One-on-ones are usually behind closed doors, and that is where we go into their personal progress and how they are doing. It is done as often as needed. You will not pull them in weekly, but you have to do it for your top key players as well as your bottom. You do not want to just keep bringing up the same issues.

If I were to describe the sales meeting, it is where we make our impact. Everyone is motivated to a certain extent, but that's where we turn the flame up, and that is where the sales leader has an opportunity to crank the heat up on the team. The heat is not the heat under their rear end, it is the motivation. It is the fire within them that pushes them.

If they are not already motivated, you cannot go in there and just motivate them all of a sudden. They have to be motivated, and they have to really want it. All you are doing is turning it up.

This is just like building anything. If any of the components are left out, it is going to come crashing down. If anything that we went through in this book is left out, the system itself will come crashing down. It is not going to be sturdy enough to hold because things happen, and that is why you want your foundation to be strong.

This is why you want this process to be nice and sturdy. We built this in such a way that as team members come and go and as markets go up and down, your system is so strong that it makes it through. You will still have a certain level of success.

Another way of looking at this is that you are given an expectation. You cannot go back and blame it on one thing or another. You cannot go back and start casting blame because you did not do your job. You cannot go back to the owner and say, "Well, the market wasn't good. This person quit on me."

Okay, what did you do about it? If your building blocks are the way that they are supposed to be, you do not have to go back and make excuses because you know what you are supposed to do. Your bench was strong, so if somebody left, someone else filled their spot.

If that market goes up and down, it is okay because you know how to ramp up your close rate to offset any market fluctuations. You know what to do.

These are your building blocks, and that is how you win.

CONCLUSION

There is a reason why they hired you in the first place, and it wasn't just so they could give you a raise.

They trusted that you would manage one of the biggest parts of the organization, and knew that you could handle the success of the organization.

I am hoping that what you are going to get out of this is the realization that the job is bigger than you ever thought it would be.

Your job is not only to bring success to the organization and the people but to understand that it is about the lives that they are changing every day.

When I say "changing lives", it is knowing that a majority of the people on their team have never been as successful as they are about to be.

Many of the people may not have even graduated from high school. They are going to graduate with a GED, but they have good work ethic, they are willing to work hard, and they are about to make more than most doctors and lawyers.

The only reason why they are going to be able to do that is because of you, their leadership, and at some point their mentor.

This gives you a higher purpose. Sales leaders feel that, again, their job is to succeed inside the organization and they just miss the bigger picture.

They miss the team.

They miss everything, and the team can see it.

The team knows when the sales leader is in it more for themselves or the company than they are for them.

It will hurt their effectiveness.

Some teams are actual teams, and then there are just teams that consist of people who are in the same space who are cohabitating until they find somewhere better to go.

Again, that sales leader is the one who sets that tone.

You have the opportunity to have a team.

You can't just say it is a team, you have to earn the team.

If you think about your coaches, your favorite coaches are also the coaches that were probably the hardest on you.

I can't think of a really good coach that I had back in the day who patted me on the back, told me how great I was, and said, "Oh, that's all right. You can try it again next time."

I can't think of a good coach that I had that was like that, who is worth talking about.

I had coaches that benched me because I wasn't trying hard enough. I had coaches that were firm, and they were tactful, but they made their point.

They didn't coddle me.

They made a good strategy and expected me to follow that strategy, but they weren't there to be my friend.

You are not there to be your team's friend.

Let's just say that you went to work for your best friend, and things got tough, and your friend had to get a little bit passionate with you. Then they said, "But it's my best friend. I don't want to find out that I hurt them. I don't want to get upset with them."

If you get too friendly with your team, it leads to relationships with no accountability.

I don't hire people to fire them. I hire people that I can fire so that if it doesn't work out, it is okay. They can be successful somewhere else. If you go in, and you start making friends with everyone, then all of a sudden you are giving them second chances and third chances, saying, "I know we can do it, I know we can pull through this." In the back of your mind you know they can't, and you know they are never going to, but you just don't want to make that call. You must keep a professional relationship.

There is a difference between a team and a family. I am not talking about your immediate family. I am talking about when they say, "Hey, our team is so close that we are like family."

I say, "I'm sorry to hear that."

The problem in most sales leadership is saying something like, "I want to treat my guys so well that they are willing to run through a brick wall for me."

This is the wrong frame of mind.

You are a servant to them.

You get to have the opportunity to change lives, and it is not so that they can go run through brick walls for you.

You need to give tough love when tough love is needed, and celebrations when celebrations are needed. Everyone deserves that opportunity to feel good about themselves and to celebrate. Celebrate for a short period, then get back to it.

Now here's my final note. Every sales leader needs to have a mentor for themselves. They need to go out and find someone so that they are not out on that island by themselves.

They need other people to talk to other than the owner of the organization. Whether they are in a slump, or they want to celebrate and want to tell somebody how good they are doing, there have to be other people.

Most sales leaders don't do that, just because they don't know any other sales leaders. We have that on our Facebook page, where there are a lot of sales leaders that they can get in touch with. They can ask the questions, and they can try to find some others in the same field as them that they can bounce some ideas off of. It's time to find those mentors.

Then, if you come to the table, healthy, prepared, and ready, you will be able to set the tone.

There is already a culture in your organization, but the sales leaders are the ones that lead people through it. It is the sales leader who can create a culture of drive, accountability, and work ethic.

Now, when I say, set the tone. I mean, really be a voice within the organization. Learn the training and the system as if it were your own.

Many sales leaders wait for someone else to train their people. It's okay to use videos, motivational quotes, and other content that does not belong to them. You must use these as tools and not the only training you provide.

You can bring in supporting material when you are training on a certain subject. However, you should know it by heart.

When your sales reps and people see the passion that comes out of you, not just out of some corporate manual, they will line up behind you to take that castle.

Now, get to work.

About the Author

Chuck Thokey is a well-known international speaker, entrepreneur, and sales and leadership coach who has worked with more than 3,000 sales leaders from around the world. Following an early career as an aerospace engineer at Bombardier / LearJet, Chuck has worked to build sales teams for countless organizations, and he is the co-founder of Top Rep High Performance Sales Training, which works with home improvement organizations to dramatically grow their sales. He lives and works in Kettering, Ohio.

Find out more about Chuck and the team at TOP REP High Performance Sales training at TopRepTraining.com

www.ingramcontent.com/pod-product-compliance
Lightning Source LLC
LaVergne TN
LVHW052336100826
845147LV00020B/1083